Spiritu

Steve Pierson

Copyright © 2023

All Rights Reserved

To my wife Tricia and my children; Makenna Trevor and Emma. Thank you for your patience. The accounts in this book took a lot out of everyone.

To the victims who have suffered under abusive church leadership, God sees your pain and carries your wounds. Grace, mercy, and justice follow in his steps!

Table of Contents

Foreword 7

Preface 19

Introduction 24

Chapter 1 26

Chapter 2 42

Chapter 3 61

Chapter 4 76

Chapter 5 93

Chapter 6 112

Chapter 7 127

Chapter 8 143

Conclusion 162

Foreword

I want to, first of all, say that Steve has written from the very core of his transformed, inner man in sharing that which God, not any man, made real His Eternal Word of Truth with regard to the subject of false, deceived, and narcissistic centered men or women who are assuming the role of pastoral leadership in a church. Thus, I want to fully recommend, without any reservation at all, the promulgation and reading of *Spiritually Abused* among the body of Christ throughout the world, let alone in the United States. This is an issue that has always been a part of the Church from its very beginning, not to mention the false prophets and ungodly priests that are seen and described in the Old Testament, which would include those who wanted to build the "tower of Babel" in Genesis 11:1-9. As you read that specific portion of Scripture, 11:4 is the key to understanding the motive behind the desire to construct that "tower": "They said, 'Come, let us build for ourselves a city, and a tower whose top will reach into heaven, and let us make for ourselves a name; otherwise we will be scattered abroad over the face of the whole earth'" (Genesis 11:4 NAU). The two phrases that are key in this verse are, "let us build for ourselves a city and a tower," and "let us make for ourselves a name," as both of these phrases express an intense, narcissistic motivation, which may clearly be seen as an attempt at "self-deification," wherein they become the final authority out of their own thinking of what is right and wrong and good and evil. This is indeed what Satan, through the embodiment of the serpent, tempted Eve with in the Garden of Eden:

> *Now the serpent was more crafty than any beast of the field which the LORD God had made. And he said to the woman, "Indeed, has God said, 'You shall not eat from any tree of the garden'?" 2 The woman said to the serpent, "From the fruit of the trees of the garden we may eat; 3 but from the fruit of the tree which is in the middle of the garden, God has said, 'You shall not eat from it or touch it, or you will die.'" 4 The serpent said to the woman, "You surely will not die! 5 "For God knows that in the day you eat from it your eyes will be opened, and you will be like God, knowing good and evil." 6 When the woman saw that the tree was good for food, and that it was a delight*

to the eyes, and that the tree was desirable to make one wise, she took from its fruit and ate; and she gave also to her husband with her, and he ate. 7 Then the eyes of both of them were opened, and they knew that they were naked; and they sewed fig leaves together and made themselves loin coverings. (Genesis 3:1-7 NAU)

Consequently, every human being born into this world from the time of the "Fall of Mankind" up through today, and until Revelation 20-22 are fulfilled, the root of our corrupted nature is the "self-deification" essence of our innate being that is the manifestation of our narcissistic "self-glorification" focus throughout our lives.

Therefore, as we look back at Genesis 4:11, the two phrases that I pointed out ("let us build for ourselves" and "let us make for ourselves") fully manifest the innate, corrupted desire of our narcissistic, "self-deification" and "self-glorification," as the two, separate verbs, "let us build" and "let us make," in Hebrew are called a "cohortative." The "cohortative" is used to express a strong desire and determination whereby one may accomplish a certain action, and along with the prepositional phrase in these two clauses, "for ourselves," the focus is unequivocally that of "self-aggrandizement," and that is especially so with the "cohortative" statement, "let us make for ourselves a name."[1] That is, "let us make a name for ourselves" that others will exalt, magnify, and deify above every other name, and indeed, that is exactly what Pastor Steve is quite accurately and clearly pointing out with regard to abusive, narcissistic, and self-centered pastors, who in turn see themselves as THE FOCUS and THE ONLY MEANS whereby people can think they are hearing God's Eternal Truth, but in truth, they are hearing a tragic, misdirected, man-centered message, versus a Christ-centered and true, Biblical message!

As I read through Pastor Steve's book, one of the passages that continually kept coming to my mind with

---

[1] E. Kautsch, ed., *Gesenius Hebrew Grammar*, 2nd ed., trans. A. E. Cowley (Oxford: The Clarendon Press, 1910; 15th printing, 1980), 319; J. Weingreen, *A Practical Grammar for Classical Hebrew*, 2nd ed. (Oxford: The Clarendon Press, 1959; Ninth impression, 1979), 88; Page H. Kelley, *Biblical Hebrew: An Introductory Grammar* (Grand Rapids: William B. Eerdmans Publishing Company, 1992), 132; Ronald J. Williams, *Williams Hebrew Syntax*, 3rd ed., rev. John C. Beckman (Toronto: University of Toronto Press, 2007), 79.

regard to everything he was saying is found in the book of I Peter:

> *Therefore, I exhort the elders among you, as your fellow elder and witness of the sufferings of Christ, and a partaker also of the glory that is to be revealed,[2] shepherd the flock of God among you, exercising oversight not under compulsion, but voluntarily, according to the will of God; and not for sordid gain, but with eagerness; nor yet as lording it over those allotted to your charge, but proving to be examples to the flock. And when the Chief Shepherd appears, you will receive the unfading crown of glory. You younger men, likewise, be subject to your elders; and all of you, clothe yourselves with humility toward one another, for GOD IS OPPOSED TO THE*

---

[2] Frederick William Danker, ed., *A Greek-English Lexicon of the New Testament and Other Early Christian Literature*, 3rd ed. (Chicago and London: The University of Chicago Press, 2000), 519.

PROUD, BUT GIVES GRACE TO THE HUMBLE. (1 Peter 5:1:-5 NAU)

Verses 2 and 3 are pivotal with all that Pastor Steve has written, but verse 3 in particular deals with the essence of the "self-aggrandizement" of those men and women who simply use their flock for their own narcissistic identity and do so through the opposite of what I Peter 5:3 is warning about – that is, they do "lord," their pastoral position "over" their flock, and they do that by misdirected, distorted, and utterly imbalanced teaching, which indeed can be "false teaching," in order that the "sheep" in his church will see him as the ONLY MOUTH through which they can hear the true teachings of Scripture. The actual word in Greek for "lording over" expresses the following meaning: "to bring into subjection, to become master, gain dominion over, subdue, and to rule over someone or something." In other words, abusive pastors are the very antithesis of what Jesus calls us to be as leaders, teachers, and examples of true, genuine discipleship to Jesus Christ, as the following passages indicate:

> *Then Jesus spoke to the crowds and to His disciples, saying, "The scribes and the*

Pharisees have seated themselves in the chair of Moses; therefore all that they tell you, do and observe, but do not do according to their deeds; for they say things and do not do them. They tie up heavy burdens and lay them on men's shoulders, but they themselves are unwilling to move them with so much as a finger. But they do all their deeds to be noticed by men; for they broaden their phylacteries and lengthen the tassels of their garments. They love the place of honor at banquets and the chief seats in the synagogues, and respectful greetings in the market places, and being called Rabbi by men. But do not be called Rabbi; for One is your Teacher, and you are all brothers. Do not call anyone on earth your father; for One is your Father, He who is in heaven. Do not be called leaders; for One is your Leader, that is, Christ. But the greatest among you shall be your servant. Whoever exalts himself shall be humbled; and whoever humbles himself shall be exalted. (Matthew 23:1-12 NAU)

They came to Capernaum; and when He was in the house, He began to question them, "What were you discussing on the way?" But they kept silent, for on the way they had discussed with one another which of them was the greatest. Sitting down, He called the twelve and said to them, "If anyone wants to be first, he shall be last of all and servant of all." (Mark 9:33-35 NAU)

And there arose also a dispute among them as to which one of them was regarded to be greatest. And He said to them, "The kings of the Gentiles lord it over them; and those who have authority over them are called 'Benefactors.' But it is not this way with you, but the one who is the greatest among you must become like the youngest, and the leader like the servant. For who is greater, the one who reclines at the table or the one who serves? Is it not the one who reclines at the table? But I am among you as the one who serves." (Luke 22:24-27 NAU)

He who corrects a scoffer gets dishonor for himself, And he who reproves a wicked man gets insults for himself. Do not reprove a scoffer, or he will hate you, reprove a wise man and he will love you. Give instruction to a wise man and he will be still wiser, teach a righteous man and he will increase his learning. The fear of the LORD is the beginning of wisdom, And the knowledge of the Holy One is understanding. (Prov. 9:7-10 NAU)

In the quote from Matthew 22:1-12, when Jesus says not to call someone "Rabbi, Teacher, Father, or Leader," He is focusing on the exaltation of men by others to a place of "semi-deification," versus focusing on Him as the source of our spiritual rebirth and the Eternal Truth of God's Word that comes through Him by means of the Holy Spirit, versus mere, flawed, skewed men, which is what we all are. Indeed, in the following two passages, we see the absolute and utter misdirection of exalting any man as the source of our truth and our spiritual identity, in turn, becoming our identity with that particular man, VERSUS JESUS ALONE:

As for you, the anointing which you received from Him abides in you, and you have no need for anyone to teach you; but as His anointing teaches you about all things, and is true and is not a lie, and just as it has taught you, you abide in Him. (I John 2:27 NAU)

And I, brethren, could not speak to you as to spiritual men, but as to men of flesh, as to infants in Christ. I gave you milk to drink, not solid food; for you were not yet able to receive it. Indeed, even now you are not yet able, for you are still fleshly. For since there is jealousy and strife among you, are you not fleshly and are you not walking like mere men? For when one says, "I am of Paul," and another, "I am of Apollos," are you not mere men? What then is Apollos? And what is Paul? Servants through whom you believed, even as the Lord gave opportunity to each one. I planted, Apollos watered, but God was causing the growth. So then neither the one who plants nor the one who waters is anything, but God who causes the growth. Now he who plants and he who waters are one, but each will receive his own reward according to his own labor. For we are God's fellow workers; you are God's field, God's building. (I Corinthians. 3:1-9 NAU)

The above passage in I John 2;27 focuses on the cult of the Gnostics, which emphasizes the fact that their illuminated teachers were the ONLY ONES who could teach the truth and that no other individuals had the ability to understand that truth except through them.[3] Thus, John was stating that without any equivocation, NO MAN, or GROUP OF MEN are our source of God's Eternal Truth, but rather, the Holy Spirit, who is in every born-again believer in Jesus Christ, is the One Who is our ultimate teacher, and He alone is the One we must seek after in understanding the truths of God's Eternal Word of Truth!

As I conclude this Forward, I want to set forth three positions concerning an abusive pastor or leader in a church: (1) If this person is a true, born-again believer in Jesus Christ, my prayer is that he or she will be brought to a disciplined brokenness by the Lord, so that in their repentance, true and

---

[3] A. M. Renwick, "Gnosticism," in *The International Standard Bible Encyclopedia, Revised*, ed. Geoffrey W. Bromiley (Grand Rapids: William B. Eerdmans Publishing Company, 1979-1988), 488.

genuine healing and restoration will occur (Hebrews 12:4-11); (2) If this person is not a true, born-again believer in Jesus Christ, my prayer is that God, by the power of the Holy Spirit, will be convicting them of their sin, the righteousness of Jesus, and the eternal Hell that awaits them if they ultimately reject Christ, and that the Lord will "draw" them to the point where they will make a genuine commitment of their life to Jesus Christ as their Lord and Savior (John 16:8-11; 6:44; Romans 10:8-13); (3) If, however, the abuser rejects either of the first two objectives, then my prayer is that the spiritual, mental, intellectual, and emotional eyes of the "abused" will be open, resulting in their leaving the unquestionable "darkness" of the abuser's presence, and in turn, being led by the Holy Spirit, become a part of a Christ-centered, Bible believing, and surrendered to the Lordship of Jesus Christ fellowship of true, born-again believers in Jesus Christ.

God bless you, Justin T. Alfred

Preface

"The thief comes only to steal and kill and destroy. I came that they may have life and have it abundantly. I am the good shepherd. The good shepherd lays down his life for the sheep."

– John 10:10-11

You might be wondering what kind of a book bares the title, "Spiritually Abused?" It almost sounds like a marketing ploy to create curiosity in the would-be reader. You might also be wondering what kind of a person would write such a book. The mentally unstable? Perhaps a person who is bored with his own thoughts? Maybe a person looking to entertain himself by writing about fringe topics that pertain to some sort of weird spiritual sub-culture? No, none of the above. On the contrary, I'm quite normal. I'm also not so bored that I'm looking to fill my time by writing about things that don't matter. The truth is this is the first book I've ever written. The only experience I have with writing is my weekly sermon preparation. I've been a Christian for thirty years and a pastor for twenty-three of those years. I don't consider myself an intellectual or a theologian, just a normal Jesus lover. I'm passionate about the Bible and, more specifically, the application of the Bible to everyday life. I believe deeply in the transforming power of the Holy Spirit and his ability to change the way a person thinks and subsequently lives. From the first days of my new life in Christ, I've always been drawn toward apologetics. I believe that every Christian needs to know how to give an answer to people who ask about their faith. I also believe that knowing the Bible keeps us from being deceived by false teaching and helps us identify false teachers. I've studied long hours over the years, preparing my mind with the necessary information to know the difference between truth and error. If I'm being honest, in my early years as a Christian, there was arrogance about me. The arrogance, coupled with the insatiable desire to argue and be right, made for a horrible apologist, not to mention a lousy Christian.

Over the years, I've witnessed a lot of examples from pastors on how to live and lead. I've seen some amazing people with incredible leadership skills direct ministries and pastor churches. I've seen leaders with such love for people that they would lay down their life for them. I've watched men and women commit themselves to the spiritual health of another, costing them their own time and money. I've been privileged to have mature Christians invest in me, expecting nothing in return. I've been blessed to see the most generous followers of Christ make the dreams of the less fortunate possible. However, I've also had the unfortunate experience of witnessing the exact opposite. I've seen Christian leaders and pastors lead with cruelty that if it weren't for their profession of faith, you would think they were an unbeliever. I've witnessed dishonesty coming from those you would expect to be advocates for truth. I've seen shepherds that are called to care for the sheep, fleece them and use them for their own gain. I've stood by and watched innocent people's reputations ruined so a church leader's bad reputation could be saved. Indeed, I've seen enough evil in the place where there is supposed to be good that if it weren't for the power of Christ to keep me, I would walk out the doors and never come back.

I set out to write this book because the church of Jesus Christ is a beautiful bride. Even with all her imperfections, she's adorned in white, clean, and pure. The ugliness of her sin is only seen if you peek beneath the garments of grace provided by her perfect groom. Jesus knows what's under those garments. He died to ensure her coverings were never removed. He lives to point her to a future, both near and far. The hope for the near is that she would be made holy. The promise for the far is that she will be made perfect. To direct her in her desire to be holy, he has given his word. To aid her in understanding his word, he has given her shepherds. The shepherds are to ensure her safety while watching over her progress towards holiness. When a pastor or church leader forgets their place and sets aside their call to serve the church and instead begins to rule it, spiritual abuse is born. Abusive cultures are formed, and unbiblical behavioral expectations begin to control the people. The unsuspecting victims are oblivious to the abuse because the masses have accepted it as "holy."

I have had the unfortunate experience of living through such abuse. It wasn't simply a person but an entire church culture that was abusive. Those of us under its influence were clueless. We had no idea that we were incrementally being trained by a culture to think in certain ways, which led to a deception that demeaned the people we were supposed to be serving.

There is no shortage of books on the market that address spiritual abuse. There are some fantastic resources available. However, what is scarce is material on how church cultures are built and used to control the people. Abuse which comes from a culture is much harder to recognize than that which comes from an individual. The reason is that the culture includes the masses. When the masses are all marching in step with one another, the assumption is that everyone is going in the right direction.

I wrote this book because spiritual abuse is a devastating reality within the body of Christ. There are many people's stories that are accounted for within these pages. There are countless tears shed by all the contributors. My hope in writing this is that the reader will be better equipped to identify not just the abusive leader, but the culture he establishes and weaponizes against the Bride of Christ.

Introduction

Nobody ever plans on joining a church family in hopes that should they leave, they'll be more spiritually damaged than when they arrived. There is an expectation that although people's experiences might include difficulty, the church wants the best for them. There's a common understanding that the church exists to help its members, not hurt them.

What happens when a church becomes unhealthy? The most obvious answer is that its attendees become unhealthy. After all, the church isn't a living entity apart from the people; rather, it draws its life from the people. If a church becomes unhealthy, it's only because its leaders have become unhealthy. Spiritually abusive churches are such for two reasons; first, everyone agrees to the abuse. Second, the abuse is propagated by an abuser. Those that agree to the abuse are doing so by submitting to a culture where certain expectations control their behavior. Oh, to be sure, no one recognizes it as abuse; nevertheless, it is. As the abuse travels through the church hidden within the culture, it trains people how to think and react to life around them. Working behind the scenes of the abusive culture is always an abusive leader. There is no such thing as an abusive church culture without an abuser controlling it. That's not to say that the abuser always acts with intention since much of what he builds is built out of ignorance. He often constructs from his unhealthy past experiences, not from a desire to damage people. Nevertheless, the culture he builds still drives the abuse.

How does a person identify an abusive church culture? How would a person know what an abusive leader looks like or sounds like? The book before you highlights four main areas where abuse often hides itself. You'll quickly discover the suggestive power of an abusive culture. You'll see how Godly, well-meaning people subject themselves to spiritual danger without realizing it. You'll also discover the manipulative tactics used to control people in the church. Finally, you'll see how escaping an abusive church and its controlling influence is possible.

For some, this may prove to be a painful read. If you have had the unfortunate experience of being a part of an abusive church or under the direction of an abusive leader, this book will no doubt bring some haunting memories to the surface. So, let me encourage you with this; "Take every thought captive to the obedience of Christ." Your past experiences and the trauma that accompanies them no longer have power over you! Enjoy your read!

Chapter 1

A Culture of Seduction

"Nevertheless, I have this against you: You tolerate that woman Jezebel, who calls herself a prophet. By her teaching she seduces my servants into sexual immorality and the eating of food sacrificed to idols."

- **Revelation 2:21**

Seduction is defined as "drawing" or "luring away." The term is used more broadly as a synonym for the act of charming someone–male or female–by an appeal to the senses. Consequently, seduction typically has a carnal connotation to it and is used most often in a sexual context. However, scripture indicates that there is a spiritual element to seduction as well. It happens when a person is "drawn away" and lured into abandoning their loyalty to God and giving it to an idol instead. In Revelation 2:20, we are introduced to a devilish type of seduction. It's a seduction that uses authority cloaked in religion to strip a person of their devotion to God. It lures its victim into a place where human authority becomes an idol. This type of seduction leaves its victims clueless as to what's happening while it's happening. Since it's religious in nature, the seducer can charm his or her victims by appealing to their spiritual senses. Much like the effects of the date rape drug Rohypnol, the victim is powerless because they're unaware of what's happening. When the seduction ends, the victim is left feeling abused and shamed. The question that arises is an obvious one: how can a person be spiritually abused by a seductive leader and abandon all spiritual discernment as well as plain common sense?

In 2003 Disney came out with its classic animation – The Incredibles. Fifteen years later, in 2018, they released the long-awaited sequel – Incredibles 2. The movie is centered around a desire that some people had to bring the retired superheroes out of hiding and allow them to start helping people again. However, there were those that didn't want the superheroes to come back. So, the villain devised a plan. Coming up with special glasses, when the glasses were placed over the eyes of the superheroes, their powers were rendered useless. All of their might and strength were not gone, just controlled. When the glasses were placed over their eyes, what they saw, thought, and did, was controlled. If the glasses were on, the villain was able to manipulate them. However, when the glasses were taken off, it was the villain who was rendered powerless, lost control, and ultimately self-destructed. And the superheroes? They regained their strength and moved on to do "super" things again.

"Spiritual seduction" is something that most abusive leaders have come to lean on as a means of control. Like carnal seduction, the abuser creates a "mood" where the abused lower their guard. Once the abused feel safe in their surroundings, they are more likely to yield to their abuser's suggestions. The "mood" the abusive leader creates is the culture that surrounds the people. Like the glasses placed over the superhero's eyes, the abusive culture controls what people see, how they think, and how they act. As long as the people in the church "wear the glasses," the seducer has control. However, if the people can get free from the culture that controls them, the abuser is rendered powerless. At the center of this seductive culture are fear and intimidation.

In John chapter nine, there was a blind man who received his sight. He was so excited; he began jumping and leaping through the temple area. He made such a commotion that it attracted the attention of the Pharisees. The Pharisees were those ultra-spiritual hypocrites that burdened everyone around them by calling people to a life they themselves weren't willing to live. When the Pharisees saw the blind man was able to see, they went to his parents to confirm his blindness and his healing. When they approached the parents and asked how their son was made well, the parents refused to answer. We're told in John 9:22 it was because they feared the Jews and the possibility of being put out of the synagogue. The Pharisees had created a culture that was ruling people through fear. They were worried about what might happen if they didn't comply with the expectations established by their spiritual leaders. The culture of fear was the weapon of abuse. It was the mechanism of control. Again, in John chapter twelve, Jesus was teaching the people and many of the leaders were beginning to believe. However, we're told in John 12:42 that "out of fear of the Jews," they did not confess for they did not want to be put out of the synagogue. Once again, the culture that the religious tyrants had created was dictating the thoughts and actions of those it had influence over.

Every culture has norms that tell how life is to be lived within that culture. We fashion our lives, our decisions, and even our laws around what our culture has determined is acceptable. The same is true within a church.

When an abusive leader manipulates the people through the culture he creates, it is something that has been done incrementally over time. The abuse is usually so subtle that the average spiritual eye would have a hard time detecting it. Add to that the spiritual vernacular that always accompanies this behavior, and one could argue it's next to impossible to see in its early stages. This seductive ploy appeals to the spiritual senses of a person. The mood, unlike physical seduction, is not created by playing romantic music but by quoting scripture. People are seduced into trusting the leader and abandon their own spiritual discernment in the process. Unquestioned loyalty to the leader is portrayed as honorable, holy, obedient, and Biblical. This is what makes this type of seduction diabolical. It uses the trust that a person should have for their spiritual leader as outlined in scripture and imposes a borderless devotion to all that he might say or suggest. Essentially, to be obedient to God is to be obedient to all that the leader says. The leader's opinions become fact and his arguments become inscrutable. To disagree only shows you are unleadable, unteachable, and do not understand leadership. When this ideology is infused into the culture of a church, people's spirituality is determined by whether or not the leader can trust their devotion to him. Covenants are created and contracts are signed, attempting to secure loyalty to the leader and his expectations built into the culture of the church. Consequently, the boundaries outlined in the Bible for submission to church authorities are ignored. The abusive leader sets up different boundaries in their place that give him the authority to interpret the scriptures meant to protect the congregant from tyrannical oversight of their faith. When this happens, the effectiveness of the culture's seduction can be seen by the degree to which the leader has "captured a person's heart." What's unfortunate is that this type of loyalty is passed off as good and holy rather than what it really is – idolatry. What do these incremental stages of seduction look like and sound like in the process of building an abusive culture? Consider the following story:

> *One day, Max and Larry were at lunch talking about the monthly church schedule. Being a young church, the two often met for such discussions to ensure things were kept on track. Max had recently returned from a mission trip to southern Mexico, and while he was gone, he left his assistant Larry in charge of the church. Max had also given Larry a list of things he wanted to be done by the time he got back. As the two spoke about the calendar, Max began to steer the conversation in a different direction. He told Larry that he was stumbled by his actions while he was gone away in Mexico. Larry looked confused as Max began to expound. Max was offended that Larry did not finish*

the list of things that were given to him. The offense was due to the fact that Larry had wanted to bless Max by surprising him with some things that Max had wanted to be done for over a year. Larry's intentions were to complete the list, as well as the extra things he knew would bless Max. When Larry ran out of time and was not able to finish all of Max's list before he returned, Max became upset. As Max explained his concern, Larry acknowledged that he should have done Max's list first and then, if he had time, finished the extra things he knew would bless Max. However, it was Max's response that puzzled Larry.

After apologizing and realizing he should have done it differently, Larry was told by Max that he had a "rebellious spirit" and that rebellion is like "the sin of witchcraft." Larry was told by Max that this type of rebellion is what Korah, Dathan, and Abiram were guilty of in opposing Moses. When Larry heard this, he responded by telling Max that the motives being applied to his heart were neither fair nor accurate. He stated his true motive was to bless Max, not rebel against him. Max pushed back, stating that Hebrews 13:17 tells a person to come under and submit to their leaders and that Larry's response in not acknowledging Max's assessment of his actions was in itself a sign of rebellion and confirmation that he didn't fully understand leadership. Larry was blown away by what seemed to be an overreaction on Max's part, a preoccupation with authority, and a blatant misuse of scripture. He knew something wasn't right with Max's response. However, Larry ignored the sense he got and excused Max's conduct out of fear of being further portrayed as "rebellious."

This story has all the essential ingredients of an abusive culture in the making. To begin with Max's complaint was a legitimate one. Larry did choose to depart from the list of things he was given and instead chose to do something that Max never asked him to do. Larry acknowledged this to Max and realized his wrong and the need to do it differently in the future. However, it's Max's response to Larry that gives us insight into the building blocks of an abusive culture.

First, the motive was applied to Larry's heart, which was inconsistent with Larry's explanation of his actions. Max was allowed to determine what Larry meant, not Larry! Max had concluded that Larry's actions and motives were rebellious, whereas Larry was looking at the situation as an opportunity to bless Max. Since he held the position of authority over Larry, Max viewed his assessment as the correct one and dismissed Larry's explanation as an additional act of the rebellion he was being accused of. Do you see what happened? Max set up a self-preservation method of reasoning that ensured he would always be right. If Max determined that Larry had sinned and that any explanation to the contrary was also a sin, then Larry's only option in obeying God was to obey Max.

One of the signs of an abusive culture is that it protects the judgments of its leaders from ever being questioned. If those judgments are questioned, the abuser will say it's only because the questioning comes from a rebellious heart. When this type of reasoning is allowed to embed itself into the psyche of the masses, what emerges is a damaging cultural norm. The people begin to operate under the assumption that the leader's position is the right one, the

Biblical one. Although nobody would dare verbalize that the leader's assessments are infallible, the culture does. Consequently, the people voluntarily surrender their spiritual discernment, the very thing God gave them as protection against being deceived. The masses remain quiet when they see questionable behavior or beliefs because it's understood within the culture you don't challenge the leader. The people are seduced into believing this because the abuser uses scripture out of context to defend it. This is what Max did to Larry.

Larry's "rebellion" was likened to Korah, Dathan and Abiram. However, Larry's situation could not have been more different. Korah, Dathan, and Abiram rebelled against Moses' leadership by convincing 250 leaders, as well as all the people of Israel, that Moses wasn't God's only chosen vessel. Moses responded by telling the people to meet him the next day, and God would choose who his leader was. This was a rebellion that had, at its root, a purpose to usurp Moses' leadership. One could even argue that they wanted to replace him all together and appoint someone to take them back to Egypt. Is that what Larry did? Larry told Max that the motives behind his actions were intended to bless him. Larry called to mind something Max had wanted months earlier and wanted to surprise him. His intentions were still to get Max's list done, but he ran out of time. This is far different from the scripture Max used in his attempt to persuade Larry that he was guilty of a rebellion tantamount to witchcraft or similar to Korah, Dathan, and Abiram.

Another sign of an abusive culture is that it idolizes its misuse of the Bible. Those guarding the abusive culture pride themselves on their devotion to scripture and use it to enforce their tyrannical rule over the church. What often sounds like a reasonable and accurate application of scripture is actually a misuse when a person takes a closer look. In the narrative, Max used Hebrews 13:17 to establish his biblical authority over Larry and Larry's obligation to submit to Max's judgements. Hebrews 13:17 says,

> *"Obey your leaders and submit to them, for they are keeping watch over your souls, as those who will have to give an account. Let them do this with joy and not with groaning, for that would be of no advantage to you."*

It's true that God has established leadership in the church and such leadership is to be recognized and respected. It is also true that when we choose to be a part of a local church, we are placing ourselves under the spiritual oversight of its leaders. We agree to submit to their direction and vision for that local church. We are also putting ourselves under their teaching, interpretation, and application of God's Word. However, a church's leadership is not the final authority for instruction and direction in a person's life – scripture is! Judging the motives of men's hearts is not a right given to any church leader, nor are their opinions and assessments to be placed on par with the authority of scripture! A leader in the church must recognize that whatever authority he claims from scripture, it is scripture that has the final authority over him. The reality of Hebrews 13:17 must always be read in light of Hebrews 13:7, which says;

> *"Remember your leaders, those who spoke to you the word of God. Consider the outcome of their way of life and imitate their faith."*

People are never required to submit to the authority of a church leader if that leader's life and doctrine does not reflect the imprint of God's character and truth! If that leader's life and doctrine reject the truth of scripture, then the congregant must obey God before man!

However, the most alarming part of Max and Larry's interaction is Larry's final response to Max. Larry knew Max's response wasn't right, yet he didn't say anything. Why not?

When Jesus was explaining the ministry of the Holy Spirit in John chapter 14, he said that the Holy Spirit would come from the Father to testify of Christ and "teach us all things." Later, in John 16:13, the Holy Spirit is said to lead and guide the believer into all truth. Clearly, the ministry of the Holy Spirit is to speak to the one who he indwells and lead him into truth. This is one of the beautiful aspects of the mediation found in Christ. Christ speaks to the believer himself. In that relationship, we find everything! We find the conviction of sin; as well as correction and instruction in righteousness.

When Larry felt that Max's response wasn't right, he ignored it and excused it out of fear that any further pushback would only add to Max's accusations that he was rebellious. The culture of fear and intimidation that Max had established ordered the thoughts and actions of Larry so that obedience to God took a back seat to obedience to Max! Larry was literally stripped of his God-given responsibility to speak the truth in love.

When an abusive leader creates an abusive culture, there is an understanding within that culture that if a person is thinking or feeling contrary to what has been established, it is a sin. Consequently, the abused congregant loses their identity in Christ and becomes a slave to man. This is the seduction that leads to idolatry!

How would healthy leadership have responded in Larry's situation? A loving shepherd always assumes the best of those he cares for. He also looks for teaching opportunities in the failures of those he leads. Not every failure warrants a rebuke or a correction. In fact, most failures are used by loving shepherds to administer grace before the instruction. If this is done right, the person who failed walks away encouraged but knows a better way for next time. A loving shepherd cares more about the spiritual growth of the one they're caring for than having their authority recognized or their ego stroked. Max should have asked Larry why he didn't complete his tasks, not told him that he was rebellious. This would have allowed Max to discover the truths behind what motivated Larry's decisions. Once he had that information, he would have known that Larry's actions were not rebellious, certainly not comparable to Korah, Dathan and Abiram. Max should have encouraged Larry by pointing to his thoughtfulness in remembering something that Max had long forgotten. He should have pointed to specific things he appreciated about Larry's surprise. Once Larry knew that the good had been recognized, Max would have had a teaching opportunity that could have gone something like this.

"Larry, I really appreciate what you did. It looks fantastic. I am blessed that you remembered something I wanted to be done so long ago. That was thoughtful. But next time, could you do me a favor? Could you finish the list I gave you first and then do the extra stuff that you wanted to bless me with? Or, just give me a quick call or text and let me know what you want to do so I know what to expect when I get home."

Faithful shepherds should be intentional about building cultures that lift people up and promote the gracious character of God! Seducing or luring people away from loyalty to the Lord and putting loyalty to man in its place is wrong. It's unholy. It's Idolatry!

Chapter 2

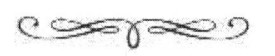

A Culture of Fear

> ***"We can easily forgive a child who is afraid of the dark, the real tragedy of life is when men are afraid of the light."***
>
> **- Plato**

It was a beautiful sunny day as the two men walked along the roadside. Both were filled with joy. Everything was as it should be. Their enemy was defeated, their nation was united, and their family and friends enjoyed the safety of living in a place where God was their protector. The two laughed and embraced as they expressed gratitude towards one another. As they approached the city on their way home, they could hear music in the background. It seemed the people were as excited as they were. The closer they got to the city, the louder and clearer the music became:

> *"Saul has slain his thousands and David has slain his ten thousands."*

Fear is a powerful sedative that numbs the spiritual senses of a believer. It often motivates the human heart to gravitate towards spaces where divine direction gives way to human reasoning. When fear is present and reigning in a believer's life, faith is not. One of the most noticeable yet hidden things in an abusive church culture is fear. When a culture is inundated with fear, not only is the abusive authority the whip that maintains the control but there is always a lack of faith present. Those on the receiving end of the culture's abuse acclimate to the fear within that culture and are unknowingly robbed of the joy which comes from trusting God.

1 Samuel 18:8 says that Saul became angry when hearing the words that David had slain his ten thousand and he had only slain his thousand. Saul's anger then turned to fear as his own insecurities began to choke out any residue of faith that might have been left in his heart. What was the result of Saul's fear? To begin with, he sought diligently to end David's life. Three times Saul threw a spear at David while he was ministering to Saul. When David escaped, Saul plotted to have David killed by lying in wait at David's home. When the plot became known to David's wife, Michal, she warned David and helped him escape through a window (1 Samuel 19:12). Michal then took a pillow and some goat hair and made an image as if David were sleeping in his bed. When Saul sent his men in the morning to kill David, they discovered David had escaped in the night. However, what happens next gives us insight into how fear

within a culture controls the thoughts and actions of its people. When Saul saw that he had been deceived by David's wife, who was also Saul's daughter, he asked Michal why she had let David go. Her response tells:

"And Michal answered Saul, 'He said to me, Let me go or I'll kill you.'"

-1 Samuel 19:17

The Bible never tells us that David threatened his wife. Michal was the one who told David of her father's plot to kill him. Why, then, did Michal lie to her father? Simply put, she was as afraid of him as the rest of the people in the kingdom were. *No doubt,* she thought to herself, *What if I tell my dad the truth? What if he gets angry? What if he turns and kills me as a result?*

Saul's abusive leadership began at home. His own family experienced his wrath and intimidation. Consequently, they bowed to his culture of fear which led them to actions that otherwise would have been different. In 1 Samuel 20, Saul became enraged at his son, Jonathan, because he found out that Jonathon was helping David, whom he was trying to kill. While sitting at the dinner table, Saul threw a spear at his own son, seeking to kill him. Saul's abusive treatment of his family further instilled fear in the hearts of those in the kingdom. After all, if a man was willing to treat his own family this way, then nobody was safe.

In 1 Samuel 22:6-10, Saul continued building his culture of fear when he threatened his men, accusing them of conspiring against him. They knew of David and Jonathon's alliance, yet they didn't say anything. What were the results of Saul's threats? Doeg stepped forward out of fear and outed David, saying he saw Abimelech give him bread to eat. When Saul found out that Abimelech aided David, Saul accused him of conspiracy and killed eighty-five priests, further securing the loyalty of the people through fear. Saul's actions sent a clear message to those he led – there was a price to be paid if they didn't capitulate to the culture's expectations. In this case, the expectation was that Saul would be in the know about everything and everyone. The expectation was that if Saul hated someone, then so better his subjects.

History shows us that in every case where tyrannical government reigns, its success is dependent upon fear ruling the people. Controlling the masses often depends on the ability to sell the "what if's." People don't like uncertainty because it causes instability. If people live in the "what if's," the fear of what could happen will affect their decisions. This is what Saul's daughter experienced. In the church, it's no different. If an abusive culture exists, it is usually because fear has replaced faith. It's because an insecure leader has refused to live by faith and, instead, has allowed his insecurities to be his voice of reason. His fear is consulted far before God is. As those insecurities express themselves toward the masses, cultural norms are established. Abhorrent ideas about loyalty are birthed and accepted without question. Church congregants are taught to serve in an environment where the "what if's" lurk in the background of every person's thought life. "What if my pastor doesn't agree with this?" "What if I have a conversation with a person my pastor doesn't approve of?" "What if I take a picture with someone and it gets posted to Instagram?" The fear woven into the fabric of the culture, built by the abusive leader, becomes the bit and bridle that controls the abused. What follows is horrendous; how a person thinks about someone is filtered through how their leader thinks about that person. What a person says and the opinions they hold are considered in light of what their leader is saying and what his opinions are. Unaware to the congregant, fear grips their soul because the culture has established that there is a price to be paid for non-compliance. What does this look like in the real world?

Several years ago, a group of worship leaders was grabbing coffee at a local coffee shop between their morning services. Afterward, Garrett and Seth drove back to the church. Garrett was one of the worship leaders and Seth was one of the pastors. As the two were talking, Garrett asked Seth if he had ever thought about planting a church. Seth had moved from out of state several years earlier in hopes of planting a church when the time was right. Seth told Garrett that he felt church planting was in his future, but God hadn't given him any clear direction as to when. Garrett said that when that time comes, he and his wife, Stacy, would love to help.

Several months later, Garrett and Stacy left that church. The pastor of the church told people they left because they were in "unrepentant sin." In the months following Garrett and Stacy's departure, the pastor often talked about them. He spoke of them in staff meetings, at lunches, and on long commutes. None of what he said was good and the more he slandered them, the more evil they became in the eyes of the listener. One day at lunch, Seth asked his pastor why the situation bothered him so much. He responded by saying, "Loyalty, I value loyalty and Garrett wasn't loyal." It was at that point when Seth shared the conversation he had with Garrett several months earlier. When his pastor found out that Seth didn't immediately tell him of this conversation with Garrett, he was visibly upset. He rebuked Seth telling him he was inappropriate for not divulging he had such a conversation. Seth was taken aback by his pastor's reaction because Seth saw Garrett's comments as an encouragement for a future calling in his life. When Seth questioned his pastor's reaction, he told Seth that Garrett was being divisive, and Seth couldn't see it. He ended their lunch by telling Seth it was important that he knew about these types of conversations in the future and that further communication with

Garrett "wasn't wise." Choosing to honor his pastor's wishes, Seth distanced himself from Garrett and Stacy.

Five years later, Seth found himself working at a company where Garrett was one of the vice presidents. One day the two went out to lunch and Garrett explained why he and Stacy had left Seth's church. Seth was blown away by how different Garrett's version of the story was from his pastor's. Garrett shared some things about the domineering and sometimes dishonest leadership style of Seth's pastor. Garrett told Seth that one of the reasons for his and Stacy's departure was because of how intrusive and controlling the pastor had become. Though Seth didn't openly validate Garett's comments, he knew exactly what Garrett was talking about. After lunch, Seth sat in his car, deeply disturbed. Then, fear overtook him. He remembered the conversation five years earlier with his pastor and how he was rebuked for not divulging the conversation he had with

Garrett. Thinking to himself, "What if my pastor finds out about this conversation?" Seth began to panic. He voluntarily called his pastor and told him about his lunch with Garrett.

Seth's pastor asked for all the details of the conversation and then ended by telling Seth this; "Brother, thank you for telling me, but to be frank, it's troubling to me that you even had that lunch. Romans 16:17 tells you to avoid those who cause division, and Garrett causes division. I need to know I can trust you with the people you choose to have fellowship with. Do I have your heart on this?"

It's important to reiterate that abusive church cultures are built by abusive leaders. The abusive leader is always insecure. Like Saul, the abusive leader needs to be the center of attention. He cannot handle when a song is sung about somebody else slaying their ten thousand when he has only slain his thousand. An abusive leader, like Saul, "eyes" the one he sees as a threat, whether that threat is to his "rule" or a challenge to narratives he's created. An abusive leader needs to be in control and therefore creates a culture of fear to assist him.

In the normal world, Garrett's encouragement of Seth's church-planting aspirations would be considered a good thing, something to be celebrated. However, to Seth's pastor, Garrett's comments were a threat. They were divisive. They were the same words in the song that moved Saul to jealousy and rage. In the Narcissistic mind of Seth's pastor, Garretts' encouraging comments were interpreted as an insult. However, what stands out most in this story is Seth's "voluntary" disclosure to his pastor about his lunch with Garrett.

When the insecurities of an abusive leader are expressed to the masses, unbeknownst to the people, cultural norms and expectations are established. When Seth called his pastor to tell him about his lunch conversation with Garrett, was it really voluntary? If you had asked his pastor, he would have said, "I never told him he had to call me." But is that really true? If you remember, five years earlier, when Seth's pastor found out he didn't tell him about his conversation with Garrett, he rebuked Seth and let him know that in his world, that was unacceptable behavior. Seth's pastor established an expectation in the mind of Seth that if he was going to be faithful to God, then he had to honor his pastor's insecurities birthed out of his lack of faith. The effectiveness of this abuse was seen when, five years later, Seth "voluntarily" called his pastor, fearing that his lunch conversation with Garrett might be another occasion for rebuke.

When abusive leaders establish their expectations in the minds of the masses, a culture is formed. Once the culture is formed, it becomes the tool of abuse. Congregants don't need specific instructions from the abusive leader regarding what his expectations might be because his desires are already known and accepted as normal behavior within the culture. Consequently, the abusive culture controls the behavior of the people who end up living a version of Christianity that caters to the fears of a man rather than a devotion to God. What's unfortunate about this is that because it's the culture of which everyone is a part, the congregants do not notice what's happening to them.

The power behind this type of fear can be a paralyzing experience that divides friendships, family members, and even churches. Those held captive by this type of abuse don't realize the depths of their bondage. Yet, their skittish behavior bears witness to their captivity on many fronts. It's common for people to be afraid to be seen in pictures or have coffee with people who are at odds with their pastor or church. "Unfriending" or "unfollowing" those same "rebellious" people on social media is very common. The reason is that the abusive leader has set the expectation that there should be no contact or friendship with those he doesn't approve of. Consequently, in the mind of the abused lives, the thought, "What if I 'like' a person's post and my pastor sees it?" "What if he thinks I'm gossiping with the person he's at odds with?" "What if I'm caught having lunch with a Christian he doesn't like?" To an outsider, this seems absurd. However, to those familiar with this type of bondage, it's haunting.

The divisiveness that flows from this type of abuse is extremely damaging. Those who the abusive leader sees as non-compliant to the thoughts and ways of the culture he's built are shunned under the banner of "Biblical fidelity." Siblings are divided. Fathers and daughters are divided. Friendships are ruined. I know of one abusive situation where the pastor sat his leadership team down and wrote names in circles on a whiteboard. The names were all the people in his congregation that he felt were divisive and unresponsive to a narrative he was propagating to his church. His staff walked out of the meeting with a clear understanding of who they were allowed to associate with and who they were not.

In another situation, a pastor was shunning an individual who left his church not agreeing with the pastor's abusive style of leadership. After months of obsessively addressing the situation in his staff meetings, he let his staff know of his expectations. They were all to keep their distance from the one being shunned. None of them were to associate with the ones the pastor marked out as "divisive." He asked them all one by one, "Do I have your heart on this?"

When the meeting was over, one of the staff members asked the pastor, "What about his wife and daughter?"

The pastor responded, "When Achan sinned, his whole family was cut off." This staff member knew exactly what was expected of them from that point forward.

In another situation, an elder of a certain church was meeting a former member of that same church for coffee. This former member had lies spoken about him by the pastor and the elder was doing his due diligence in secret. The reason the meeting was in secret was because the pastor would not allow the accused to meet with his elders to answer the false accusations against him. While the two talked, a member of the church walked in and saw them both. The elder's heart was struck with fear, knowing that his meeting would be reported to the pastor. In the next elders gathering, the pastor openly rebuked this elder for defying his wishes by meeting with the former member. The abuse was directed at the "wayward" elder but also at the other leaders in the room. Every one of those leaders knew that if they failed to heed the demands of their pastor as to who they were allowed to talk to, they also would have a strong rebuke awaiting them.

Years ago, a youth pastor was holding his weekly service for his high school students. As the youth pastor was sharing his message, two students in the back row were quietly laughing but clearly not paying attention. As the pastor was talking, he abruptly stopped his message and yelled out from the top of his lungs, "HEY, YOU TWO, OUT! GET OUT, AND DON'T COME BACK!" The two students sat, shocked at the public humiliation. Making matters worse, the pastor stopped the entire service until the students stood up and took their walk of shame, leaving the sanctuary. It never dawned on this leader that privately pulling the kids aside to administer correction was the Godly thing to do. The abuse was directed not only at the disruptive students but also at the hundred and fifty other kids that sat watching and fearfully wondering what they would have to do to be publicly humiliated.

Many years ago, the Bugs Bunny cartoons featured a particular episode where Elmer Fudd, the arch enemy of

Bugs Bunny, had the power to hypnotize. After successfully using his power to make a bear act like a canary, he attempted to use the power on Bugs. When the power to hypnotize Bugs didn't work, Elmer began to cry. When Bugs asked Elmer Fudd why he was crying, Elmer responded by saying, "How can I hypnotize you if you don't cooperate?"

Fear embedded into a church culture is hypnotic. When it's allowed to take hold of the congregant's heart and mind, that congregant will cooperate with all the suggestions made by the abusive leader. The abuser will be allowed to suggest things which might seem at first to be bizarre, but with deceit, he is able to convince the people that the bizarre is normal, even holy.

I know of a situation where a pastor's wife sent a letter to her husband's board of elders exposing his ungodly conduct at home. After resigning from his position, a week later, he asked to return. What ensued was a bitter public feud which led to the resignation of all his elders, pastors, and staff, not to mention the departure of two-thirds of his congregation. When the pastor regained control of his church a year later, he stood his wife up in front of the congregation and had her renounce the letter she wrote. Essentially, he had her take the blame for the ruin of his church. When one congregant was asked what they thought about the wife "falling on the sword" for her husband, he said, "At first, it felt a little creepy. However, Pastor explained to us how this was a beautiful display of public repentance." Notice the original "gut check" in the congregant. He thought this public humiliation was "creepy." It was creepy! It was also ungodly and abusive! A husband is called to lay his life down for his wife like Christ gave himself for the church, not sacrifice her on the altar of self-preservation. What's sad is that the hypnotic state of the congregation allowed the pastor to not only get away with it but to suggest it was holy and Biblical.

In another situation, a pastor had his teenage son and his fiancé stand up in front of their congregation and confess their immoral failings. Misusing scripture, the pastor placed his congregation in a "hypnotic state," making them believe that this type of ecclesiastical abuse was holy and that public shame was the path to repentance. In a similar story, the same church leader had a couple that was dating stand up in front of the congregation during a mid-week service and confessed to pre-marital sex. Misusing James 5:16, he seduced the congregation into believing that the dating couple was obeying scripture. The pastor explained, "James 5:16 says to Confess your sins to one another…" In the abuser's twisted interpretation, this meant to stand and tell everyone your private sin. The congregation was "hypnotized" by the misuse of scripture. James 5:16 is in the context of calling for the elders of the church to anoint with oil and pray for a person if they're sick. It says, "The Lord will raise him up and if the sick have committed sin, God will forgive them. Therefore, confess your sins to one another and pray for one another so that you may be healed." The abuser convinced the church that a Biblical truth meant for healing had unilateral use in any situation the abuser saw fit.

The tragedy in both stories is that the abused bride of Christ now maintains a deep impression within her psyche. The impression is that if a person truly wants to repent, they must publicly denounce themselves before the church. For most, this unbiblical and abusive practice will serve as a deterrent to repentance because the sinner will most certainly choose to hide their sin rather than shame themselves before the assembly.

The Bible tells us plainly in Proverbs 29:25 that "the fear of man is a snare, but the one who trusts in the Lord is safe." When fear is allowed to be the hands that shape a church culture, it is the man whom people will seek to please, not God. The abusive culture set up by the abusive leader will always be designed to glorify that leader. His own insecurities and fears will tell the people how he is to be "worshiped" in that culture. This form of idolatry hides itself from the most devoted believers convincing them of the purity of their false worship. When those believers come to their senses and realize the manipulative ploys which drew them into their deception, one thing becomes more prevalent than any other – they were lied to!

Chapter 3

A Culture of Lies

"Beware of the Man of One Book"
– Thomas Aquinas

Twenty-four hundred years ago, the Greek philosopher Plato introduced his "Allegory of the Cave." In his allegory, a group of prisoners was confined to a cave where they had been since birth. They had no contact with the outside world and therefore were naive to its realities. The prisoners were chained, facing a wall with a fire burning behind them, giving off a faint glow. As people walked in front of the fire with different objects, shadows were cast onto the wall in front of the chained prisoners. The prisoners named these objects believing the shadows were reality. Suddenly, one of the prisoners was freed and left the cave. After his eyes adjusted to the sunlight for the first time in his life, he realized that the object's shadows, which were cast onto the wall he had looked at since birth, were not reality at all. The freed prisoner then returned to the cave to share his discoveries with the other prisoners. Upon arriving, the freed prisoner, having seen reality outside of the cave, had a hard time seeing the images on the wall. The prisoners, still bound, thought the journey had made the freed prisoner delusional and so they violently rejected his efforts to free them. The moral of the story is that most people are comfortable in their ignorance and are hostile to anyone who points it out.

Over the years, there has been debate as to what was meant when Thomas Aquinas coined the phrase, "Beware of the man of one book." However, most people agree that, in some way, it's referencing the danger associated with the man who thinks he has all the answers and instructs others to look no further than his one source.

Controlling the information highway in any tyrannical system is crucial. Immediately following the election of Adolf Hitler, Germany established the "Propaganda Ministry." Hitler understood that any freedom to access information contrary to what the Third Reich distributed could undermine his cause. Consequently, newspapers, printing presses, television, and radio were all ceased and brought under government control. The people were only going to know what Hitler wanted them to know. Any pursuit of information other than what the government provided would lead to alienation and, quite possibly, confinement in a concentration camp.

As mentioned in the last chapter, every abusive leader is insecure. Those insecurities are seen by the congregation but rarely recognized as such. In fact, one of the most powerful things about an abusive church culture is that it manipulates information in a way that makes the abusive leader seem stronger and holier than he actually is. Like driving into a fog bank, an abusive leader takes advantage of the culture he's built by clouding the judgments and perceptions of those he leads. In his mind, his strength depends on how the people view him rather than how God views him. To that end, he lies to create false narratives. He manipulates information to convince the people of what he wants them to see and hear. Much like the Wizard of Oz, he hides behind the curtain, separating reality and fantasy, while he leads with smoke and false impressions. When a person finally comes out from underneath the control of an abusive culture, their eyes are opened. It's as if the curtain has been pulled back and they realize that Oz is simply a deceptive man. Like the freed prisoner from Plato's cave, they realize that what they had been looking at the entire time wasn't real.

Proverbs 18:17 says, "The one who states his case first seems right, until the other comes and examines him." The Bible is replete with instructions to the believer to guard themselves from deception. Jesus himself put the responsibility on his disciples to see to it that they were not led astray by those who came in Christ's name (Matt 24:4). When Paul and Silas shared the truth of God in the synagogues at Berea, we're told that the Berean's were noble because they examined what they were told in light of scripture. The New Testament church itself was protected against those who would bring an accusation against another person without sufficient evidence. In Matthew 18:16, we're told that when an offended brother could not personally settle a matter with the person he was accused of wrongdoing, that brother was to take "one or two" witnesses with him. The purpose was so that every accusation could be established. Deuteronomy 19:15-17 tells us that the "one or two witnesses" were to be leaders in office who were charged with looking carefully into the accusations. We're told that part of their responsibility was to set both people down in the controversy and hear from both parties. Essentially, the accuser would state his case and the accused would have the opportunity to answer. Those in office would then investigate by gathering all the information and presenting a judgment. The point is obvious, the Bible teaches that no one person is to control all the information. The Bible teaches that no one person's opinions are to be taken as fact. Furthermore, the Bible commissions the individual believer to protect himself from deception by making sure he has all the information available before making a decision (Proverbs 18:13).

In an abusive church culture, the leader maintains control of the people by maintaining control of the information they receive. If a person has access to information outside of what the abusive leader offers, that information might challenge the narrative of the abuser and, in turn, threaten his ability to control. This is why it is not uncommon for abusive leaders to alienate those they lead from the people that might disagree with their narrative. Such was the case with Jacob:

> *Jacob was a young man watching his church be dismantled by infighting amongst those he always knew to be friends. Jacob's pastor would often speak of people that had left his church as if they were in rebellion to God. The problem was that many of the people that Jacob's pastor implicated in this "rebellion" were people that Jacob knew to be lovers of Christ. One day Jacob decided to call one of the former pastors who had left his church to ask to meet for coffee. Jacob wanted to get this pastor's side of the story as it pertained to the reason he left Jacobs's church. When Jacob's pastor found out that he had a coffee appointment with*

someone he accused of wrongdoing, Jacob was pulled into a private meeting with his pastor. Three hours later, well into the early morning hours, Jacob's meeting ended. Shortly after, Jacob called the former pastor he was scheduled to meet with and canceled their appointment. When this pastor asked why he was canceling their appointment, Jacob said that after talking to his pastor, he realized he was being a "busybody."

The unfortunate thing about this account is that Jacob was doing the very thing scripture commands him to do. Proverbs 18:13 warns us against coming to a conclusion on a matter unless we know the whole matter. It goes on to say that taking a position without all the information is foolish and leads to shame. However, in an abusive church culture, that is exactly what happens. The abusive leader is allowed to subvert scripture. He establishes an understanding within the culture itself that the pursuit of information outside of what he provides is unbiblical and sinful. He even goes as far as to make agreements and contracts surrounding his insecurities.

Years ago, a youth pastor felt called by God to leave the church he was serving and pursue a different call at another church. Upon telling his lead pastor of this new direction God was leading him in, his pastor told him he felt his decision was a betrayal. Nevertheless, the lead pastor told the youth pastor that if he agreed to stay off social media and not make contact with a particular person who had left his church, he would pay his salary until he left. The youth pastor agreed. Upon leaving, the youth pastor decided to reach out to this forbidden contact and did return to social media. Six months later, this youth pastor was publicly denounced as "rebellious" and "divisive."

The byproduct of this type of control is that the leader is allowed to build an unchallenged narrative about people and situations. Lies can be presented as truth and misrepresentation of the facts becomes undetectable. Once the abusive leader has established himself as the most reliable source of information, the moral of Plato's allegory becomes a reality – the prisoners chained in the cave reject any and all information that might suggest that they are actually ignorant of the facts. Consequently, any source of information that might contradict the abusive leader's narrative is met with aggression. This is one of the reasons why an abusive leader fosters a divisive culture, he has no choice. To maintain control of the people he's deceived, he must control who they associate with. If the abusive leader cannot control the people who challenge the truthfulness of his narratives, then he must control what others think of them. What emerges from this type of abuse is horrifying. People's reputations are ruined and relationships end, all based on lies! Additionally, family members are shunned and faithful congregants are made to feel like they're unholy and in rebellion to God. In this type of culture, definitive lines of allegiance are drawn. People that attempt to leave are painted out to be deserters. They're called "uncommitted" and often accused of abandoning the work of God and sometimes God himself. When this type of deception reaches its apex, Satan is welcomed into the church to devour the Bride of Christ, all the while, the church sits back and applauds his abuse as "holy."

As was mentioned before, an abusive leader leads from his insecurities. It's fear and not faith that undergirds his decisions. Never is this clearer than in his pursuit and control of information. An abusive leader hates surprises! Because his control of the people is maintained through exaggerations and lies, he needs to know what information is contrary and where that information originates. It's not uncommon that when he becomes aware of a narrative contrary to his own, paranoia sets in. Consequently, pressure is applied to his demand to know what others know. A person might be asked, "Where did you hear this from?" And, "Who have you told this to?" The abuser's motivation for these questions is not to be misunderstood. What he really wants to know is who he has to contend with and who has information contrary to what he has supplied. If the person being asked refuses to answer for confidentiality reasons, they are often chided and said to be in rebellion for not submitting to their leaders. The smallest of matters become major issues. However, this narcissistic behavior does have an end game. The abusive leader hates truth! When an abusive leader obtains the information that might expose his deception, he will often use that information to adjust the story he's concocted. These "lies on the fly" are real-time adjustments meant to help him preserve his deception. When a person challenges the edited version of his story, they are often told they "misunderstood" what he originally said.

Phrases like, "That might be what you heard, but that's not what I said," or "that might be what you read, but that's not what I wrote," are used to avoid any accountability to his pre-edited version of his new reality. Simply put, the abuser says and does anything he can to avoid being proven a liar.

In recent history, there has been a lot of debate on the use of torture to obtain information. In the wake of the 9/11 attacks on the Twin Towers, it was proposed by someone that employing enhanced interrogation methods in this new war was a viable option for obtaining intelligence. The outcry over the type of torture being used during CIA interrogations of enemy combatants at Guantanamo Bay drew attention to the effectiveness of emotional and psychological manipulation. In the process of employing this type of torture, people were often secluded for long periods of time. The temperature in the room would be set at an uncomfortable level while constant borage of lying rhetoric would fill the room. The person being tortured would be denied food as well as receive a relentless attack on their psyche. The purpose of this type of torture was to break the prisoner down until he had no more emotional stamina and would volunteer information simply to escape the conditions.

When an abusive leader is seeking to maintain control of people, how he gets information, and communicates it, is often tantamount to psychological abuse. Congregants are dragged into long meetings. These meetings can last anywhere from three-four hours and often go into the next day. I know of an occasion where a pastor was invited to a congregant's house for breakfast to try and rectify a situation with their teenager. The pastor came for breakfast and didn't leave till dinner! The meeting became an 8-hour interrogation where the abusive leader tried to convince the congregant of sin they didn't commit. The goal of the abuser was to get the congregant to see things his way and to publicly pronounce their guilt in front of the church.

Additionally, those being prodded for information or told what certain information means are not only tired and hungry but also emotionally spent. People on the receiving end of the abuser's constant borage of rhetoric, and reorganization of the facts, will do anything to have it stop. It's not uncommon for a person to walk into one of these marathon meetings with information that is true, only to emerge three hours later, very confused. Some emerge, even questioning their own recollection of things. Since the abusive leader operates under these psychologically strenuous circumstances, the people are more prone to accept his "suggestions" of reality. People are actually convinced of things they don't believe. The abuser uses repetitive suggestions and faulty interpretations of facts to create his fantasy world in the mind of the one being abused. The follow-up tactic to securing these implanted lies as reality is equally deceptive. The abuser will often recall conversations that never happened, making people accountable for words they never spoke.

Additionally, Abusive leaders utilize information to protect the lies they've established through what is called "projecting." Projecting is when a person guilty of an offense (usually in secret) accuses his accuser of the same offense but does it first. The abusive leader does this in an attempt to discredit the one who might divulge damning information by making it seem like their accusations are retaliatory and, therefore, not creditable. This is why the abusive leader frantically seeks to know what people know when he believes his lying narrative may be exposed. He wants to understand what's being said so he can jump out in front with manipulation before his lies are brought to light. I once heard of a pastor who was suspected of online sexual misconduct. When his fear grasped him and he thought his misconduct might come out, he asked a fellow congregant to clean his computer. He told this congregant that he believed two former members were hacking his computer remotely and were sending inappropriate emails to members of the opposite sex. Although these former members had no access practically or experientially, the abusive pastor's "projecting" served as a protective mechanism in the event that his private sin life became known.

When an abusive leader constructs a culture that recognizes his version of reality as the most reliable and his "one book" of information as the only viable source of truth, then that culture becomes abusive. The people accept lies and distortions as facts. Since they have no way of judging the validity of those "facts" without seeking information outside of what's been provided, their judgments and decisions become destructive. They end relationships while casting judgment on every person's spiritual status except their own. Their assertion that everyone is wrong except them leads them to the same folly as Saul of Tarsus – they persecute those Christ died for. The abused become the abusers. While living in the dark, they insist they can see, and although they're invited to leave the cave, they're convinced their view of the wall is reality.

Fyodor Dostoevsky, a 19th-century Russian novelist, once said,

"Don't lie to yourself. The man who lies to himself and listens to his own lies, comes to a point that he cannot distinguish the truth within him or around him and so he loses all respect for himself and for others. And having no respect, he ceases to love."

Love is, without a doubt the most supreme Christian ethic and the greatest motivator for telling the truth. Whether that love is for God and our desire to please him or for others and our desire to have authentic relationships, love motivates a person to speak the truth. When we lie to ourselves and come to believe the new reality that our lies create around us, we lose truth from within. Deception becomes the "light" responsible for our thoughts and decisions. Our interactions with others suffer the assault that comes from the wicked one as he spreads his pain and destruction through the darkness he's convinced others to live in. When this happens, love dies. It dies because truth and love are inseparable!

Chapter 4

A Culture of Condemnation

"Steve! I told you not to wander off in this grocery store, didn't I? I'm not going to repeat myself again. Now I want you to hold on to this shopping cart and don't let go! If you take your hands off this cart, you will be in big trouble when we get home."

These were my mother's words to me many times growing up. I loved going to the grocery store. It was, in some ways, a place of freedom, as my mother's attention was momentarily pulled away. This was the place where I would find the liberty every eight-year-old desires. I would venture off onto aisle 4 while my mother resided on aisle 3. In my moment of freedom, I got to handle the merchandise I knew we would never buy. I poked the bread with my finger, ate the "free" candies from the bins on the bulk aisle, and sniffed all the laundry detergents. And the best part of this; there was no voice in the background telling me to leave things alone. However, my mother's call for me to return always brought me back to aisle 3 with haste! It was upon my return to aisle 3 that this familiar mantra was recited, "Hold on to this cart and don't let go!" I hated the shopping cart! The shopping cart was my place of confinement. It was the place of surveillance. This was where my mother had total control of me. As I held on to the front edge of the shopping cart, it was her that steered me through the aisles. If I tried to pull in a direction she didn't wish to go, she used the cart to drag me back. To this day, every time I go into a grocery store and grab a cart, I have a momentary flashback of a little boy holding on to its front edge and being controlled with its every turn.

Thus far, we have looked at several cultures that an abusive leader develops in order to control the people he leads. However, none is more devastating to the psyche of its victim than this next one - A Culture of Condemnation.

In all of what has been mentioned so far, we've seen environments that people step into. This means there is an illusion we step into when we interact with the seduction mentioned in chapter one. There is also an illusion we step into when we interact with the fear we discussed in chapter two. Finally, there is an illusion we step into when we interact with the culture of lies which we saw in chapter three. All these illusions play a part in controlling our decision-making. However, when a person finds themselves in a culture of condemnation, the danger isn't found in an illusion they're stepping into, the danger is found in what is being done to them personally. There's an assault on their soul and a battering of their mind that controls their view of proper self-worth given through the cross of Jesus Christ. This assault leaves a lasting imprint on their mind and ultimately attacks the most essential promise of their faith given to them when Jesus said, "It is finished." (The debt of sin has been paid for in full).

Control through condemnation is an extremely powerful weapon of manipulation because it uses elements of truth to undergird its attack. In Psalm 51:3, David said, "I know my sin is ever before me." At the core of the gospel is an understanding that man can never escape the reality of living with his sin in this life. It is, in essence, "Ever before him." However, we understand that what is also at the core of the gospel is that, though our sin is ever before us in life, the condemnation that accompanies it has been transferred to the son of God on the cross. This has been accomplished by God himself and is the demonstration of his gracious and merciful character. Therefore, for sinful man to pick up condemnation and use it as a weapon to control the people Christ has set free, is an attack on the person and work of Jesus Christ. This abusive act demonstrates a hostility toward the gospel, not an understanding of it. The ways this works itself out in real life can be horrifying and damaging, as was the case with Eddie.

Eddie was a young, intelligent man who grew up in a ministry-minded home. His father was a dynamic pastor who attracted the masses through his ability to articulate Biblical truth. He was looked upon as a man of integrity by those he led and had a place of prominence within the local Christian community. From the outside, his personal walk with God, his family, and his church all seemed to be a reflection of God's goodness that comes from a devotion to Biblical faith. However, behind closed doors, reality painted a different picture. His personal walk with God was filled with lies and false perceptions created to hide his own carnality. His healthy marriage was an illusion created to hide his own selfish, narcissistic behavior. Finally, the health of his church was tantamount to pre-cancerous cells left untreated growing more lethal with every passing year. In short, the distance between who he painted himself out to be to others and who he really was, was light years apart. Consequently, his relationships with those who knew who he really was were left in shambles. One of those people was his son, Eddie. Eddie loved his father dearly. Growing up, he listened to his advice and came into his own relationship with Christ as a result. However, because Eddie was a strong young man who thought for himself, there came the point where his father's control and manipulation within the home became too much. As Eddie came to discover the truth about his dad's character flaws, the contention between him and his father intensified. When Eddie's dad's gaslighting was no longer effective, he started telling others that his son was rebellious and struggling with his faith. The insidious nature of all of this came to its apex when Eddie's father told him that God had spoken, saying that his troubled marriage wouldn't be repaired until his relationship with Eddie was restored. He was suggesting that his marriage problems were due to his son's "rebellious ways," and the stress he placed on his parents. The impact of this type of emotional manipulation using condemnation as a weapon cannot be understated, nor the damage that it causes. Like every believer in Christ, Eddie was aware of his own sin. It was "ever before him." He was aware of his past failures and the effects those failures had on those around him, including his own family. However, the Bible says that the grace of God covers Eddie's sin and removes his condemnation. There is no case to be made against him; it has been dismissed. Those caring for Eddie's spiritual health would never suggest that Eddie lives in the present as a product of the past he's repented of. Additionally, any right-minded Christian man would never blame his damaged marriage on someone else. The truth is that Eddies father was trying to control him using condemnation to hold him responsible for something he had nothing to do with. To create an illusion that your righteousness is superior to someone else's so, you can gain leverage to bring them into submission isn't right. Hoping a person feels bad for something they didn't do so they'll surrender to you in a dispute is abuse. In this case, condemnation was used to infiltrate Eddie's mind, which was already sensitive to his past failures. Condemnation was used to subconsciously suggest to Eddie that his past was his present, and therefore he was the reason for his parents' marriage problems. The intended use of condemnation in Eddie's case was to suggest that his only place as the guilty, rebellious son, was to grab the front of the shopping cart and accept whatever direction he was being taken.

In Romans 8:1 the Apostle Paul states that "There is, therefore, no condemnation for those who are in Christ." These uplifting words come on the heels of a vulnerability in Romans 7, which most people can relate with. In Romans 7, Paul talks about the normal Christian experience, which plagues every believer throughout portions of their life. That is, the desire to make the right decisions which honor God but struggle and often fail to fulfill those desires. Christianity is about the long game. It's about "God who is at work in us, both to will and to work for his good pleasure" (Philippians

2:13). Holiness is a "now" and "not yet." This means that on the one hand, we're as holy as we will ever be, "seated in heavenly places in Christ Jesus" (Ephesians 2:6), having "been made the righteousness of God in Christ" (2 Corinthians 5:21). On the other hand, we are "Working out our own salvation" (Philippians 2:12), and "Pursuing righteousness" (1 Timothy 6:11). It's in our pursuit of righteousness that much of our unrighteousness is unveiled. We begin our walk with Christ having a little "swag" in our step, not realizing the depth of our depravity. As time goes by, the saving grace of God takes a far more prominent role in our spiritual disposition. It's not that God's grace becomes more effective with time, it's that our understanding of our own sinful nature develops. We live with ourselves during our most "holy" moments, and we still realize there is an ever-present draw toward sin. It is as Paul said in Romans 7:21; "I find it to be a law that when I want to do right, evil lies close at hand."

What all this translates to is an extensive list of transactions with our own sinful nature. As we move toward spiritual transformation, we're still left with the Romans 7:21 law that says evil resides in our sinful flesh. Because of this reality, any Christian can access the archives of their own unfaithfulness. They won't have to dig past their own thought life a minute before reading this last sentence. This is what it means to have our "sin ever before us." This being the case, if a believer does not grasp the truth of Romans 8:1, that "there is no condemnation in Christ," they will inevitably live a life of self-condemnation. They will think of self-condemnation to be a form of repentance rather than what it is, selfishness. Self-condemnation robs the cross of its power in a person's life. It suggests that if a person feels bad about their sin and experiences condemnation long enough, they will be qualified to receive God's grace. In such cases, self-condemnation becomes the salvific element, not the grace of the resurrected Christ. This is important to understand because people who choose to live under self-condemnation are often easy prey for the spiritual abuser. How so? Consider Rich's story.

Rich had a rough life growing up. He certainly didn't have the Christian influences that would have spared him from many of life's woes. Rich was a man who made many mistakes in his early life. When Rich received Christ as his savior, he had several regrets that he looked back on. Some of those regrets had to do with how he fathered his kids at times. Rich was a great Dad and he had amazing children that grew to love the Lord due to his witness and discipleship. Nevertheless, like many parents who come to faith in Christ later in life, it's easy to look back and wish they had done some things differently. Rich also struggled with self-condemnation. He knew about the Grace of God and even taught it to others, but he often had a hard time applying it to his own life. One day Rich got the call that every parent feared—his eldest son had died, he had taken his own life. Such a tragedy unlocks a host of thoughts; "What was the last thing I said to him?" "Did I tell him I loved him?" "Could I have done anything different to prevent this?" Rich was devastated, to say the least. To make matters worse, Richs' struggle with self-condemnation left him wondering if he had some culpability for his son's death. This tragedy left Rich extremely vulnerable and in need of a shepherd that could speak the truth and help lift him out of the condemnation that Satan was using against him. When Rich confided in his pastor, he divulged that he felt responsible because of the mistakes of his past. Rich felt, in some way, he had contributed to the emotional instability of his son at the time of his death. He told his pastor he felt his son's death was partially his fault.

This type of trauma has a way of hijacking a person's emotions. When we experience loss of this magnitude, our feelings and the conclusions they come to are very unreliable because they are formed in our pain. Any person counseling or giving advice in highly traumatic situations, such as Richs', needs to understand this. They need to know to listen but not be so quick to validate the conclusions which the grieving come to. Time often clears the mind of the hurting and allows them to process their pain differently than they did at the beginning. Therefore, the best thing a pastor can do on the heels of tragedy is just to listen. Be there for the grieving. Bear their burdens with them. Let them know they have someone to walk with. Encourage them. This is the role of a shepherd and a friend. This is what Job lacked in his greatest time of need, as his counselors only added to his agony. The worse thing for a person grieving over something as life-altering as suicide is to have someone make their misery worse. When Rich confided in his pastor, he was looking for a shoulder to cry on. He was seeking the shepherd's care. He was not asking to be told by his pastor, "Your son's death is your fault." Yes, you read that correctly. It's unimaginable to think of any human being adding to the emotional pain of another by saying such reckless and insensitive words. However, this is exactly what Rich was told. Why would any person, let alone a shepherd of God's people, tell another person such stinging and hate-filled words? The answer may shock you.

In January 2014, Garnett Spears, a five-year-old boy, was brought into the hospital by his mother, Lacey claiming he suffered from multiple seizures. After running tests, the doctors couldn't find any medical evidence to support Lacey's claims, so they ordered the discharge of young Garnett. Then suddenly, before being discharged, Garnett suffered a violent seizure. The medical staff rushed to attend to the young boy's condition. After running several tests, they noticed Garnett's sodium was at lethal levels. There was no medical explanation for his condition and not long after, the five-year-old died as a result. Garnett's passing raised immediate suspicions of foul play. The investigation that followed uncovered the horrifying truth—Garnett's mother had been poisoning him with salt since he was an infant. Lacey Spears was later convicted of second-degree murder and sentenced to twenty years to life in prison. The trial revealed that Lacey suffered from a psychological disorder called "Munchausen Syndrome by Proxy" (MBP). MBP is when a person, usually a mother, intentionally keeps their child sick. The disorder is explained by experts to be motivated by the perpetrator's extreme desire for attention. Those suffering from MBP find their identity in the sympathy and praises given to them by others for their sacrificial care of the one they made sick. It is considered abusive behavior and one of the most extreme forms of narcissism, as it feeds on creating illness in others in order to satisfy a personal desire to feel needed.

What would motivate a pastor to say the things that Rich's pastor said to him? When narcissism makes its way into church leadership, the ministry becomes infected. The subtle ways people are taught in staff meetings, discipleship groups, and private office chats are all a part of spreading the illness. Healthy people are made sick and an unhealthy dependency on the one that's making them sick is formed. Like MBP, the victims are poisoned with condemnation and then allowed to recover just enough before the next dose of condemnation is administered. This cycle is very similar to the "Love Bombing" manipulation techniques of Sun Myung Moon's Unification Church in the 1970s. This technique entailed three phases of manipulation. The first was the "Idealization stage." This stage was where the love bomber groomed their target by showering them with praises and adoration. The target was drawn into the relationship by the manipulator's care and a dependency was formed. In a ministry context, this might entail the insinuation that a person is gifted by God, and not only does the manipulator see those gifts but also plans to use those gifts. A dependency begins to form as the target believes the manipulator holds the keys to his ministerial future. However, when the target disagrees with the manipulator, the second phase of love bombing reveals itself—The Devaluation Stage.

This is where the manipulator uses the relationship, which the target values, as leverage to control the target. In this phase, the manipulator will begin to ridicule, degrade, and correct the target in such a way that the target sees the relationship might be in jeopardy. The motivation behind this manipulation is not only to establish a righteous superiority but also to draw the target back into submission out of fear of losing what they have come to value. In a ministry context, this is where condemnation becomes very effective. Assuming the idealization stage of the relationship entailed vulnerability, which it usually does, the manipulator has personal information about his target. This means that there was likely a confession of certain struggles, sins, and other sensitive information that was gathered by the manipulator under the guise of a relationship. It's not uncommon for the manipulator to assemble files on different people siting conversations the way the manipulator remembers as well as notes from the gossip of others. When the manipulator is trying to regain control of his target, he brings up this information in a condemning fashion to keep the target sick and in need of his constant care.

The power of this strategy is overwhelmingly suggestive. People confess things they're not guilty of and admit to intentions that were never their own. The intended goal of the manipulator is to give just enough condemnation so that the target will realize how sick they really are and who it is that gives them mercy and grace. This is precisely why an abusive leader often refers to themselves as the merciful and gracious party in their relational quarrels. When this works, the target falls back into line, feeling indebted to the manipulator for their compassion. The darkness surrounding this type of manipulation is insidious because the manipulator often gathers validation of their twisted version of grace and mercy from others. They essentially build a case against their target by parading the target's sickness for others to see. This is why they are so fixed on publicly addressing other people's sins. It's the ultimate form of condemnation! Church leaders, congregants, and family members are presented with condemnation dressed up as "care" in order to establish a narrative that further helps the manipulator control his target. At the same time, the manipulator is shaping his control over those same church leaders, congregants, and family members by telling them what they should think about his target. If this devaluation stage does not give the manipulator the control he seeks, the final phase of Love Bombing takes over—The Discard Phase.

This is where the target is discarded with a borage of psychological darts aimed at causing the most damage in the shortest amount of time. This comes in the form of departing letters, texts, emails, and gossip-filled conversations directed at hurting the one that can't be controlled. This is nothing short of character assassination. It is this final phase that serves as the most plausible explanation for Rich's pastor's cruel remarks.

This type of deep dive into the mind of a manipulating leader who uses condemnation as a weapon of control is demonic at its core. It's frightening to think that church leadership can operate with such dark influences disguised as Biblical care and then create an entire culture that subtly trains others to lead the same way. To be fair, this type of extreme church abuse is rare. Most spirit-filled churches have their problems associated with leading others and striking a balance between responsible shepherding and domineering dictatorship. However, the slope to a culture of condemnation is a slippery one. It begins with one fleshly motivated move to use condemnation to gain the upper hand on another person. It starts with the subtlety of recording conversations of people's vulnerable moments, then storing and eventually using those recordings at a time when you can gain the most. It's kept alive when a person establishes their moral superiority in an organization, a relationship, or a family, not by living a life above reproach but by highlighting the faults of everyone around them.

Make no mistake, when condemnation is weaponized and used by a Christian, the fallout contaminates everyone, most of all the one who used it!

Chapter 5

Escaping the Abuse

"The world will not be destroyed by those who do evil, but by those who watch them without doing anything."
― *Albert Einstein*

If you remember back in chapter 3 and the allegory of Plato's cave, there were three prisoners that were chained facing a wall. One of those prisoners got loose and found out the truth about the shadows being cast on the wall. When he came back to tell his friends, he was met with aggression and disbelief. In the end, the freed prisoner had to walk out of the cave by himself and leave his friends and former life behind. This portion of the allegory says a lot about the bondage people experience when they're part of an abusive church. This portion of the allegory shows us that it is very difficult to break free and more difficult to free others from deception. However, escaping an abusive church isn't as hard as it may seem.

In 1 Kings 22, Ahab, the king of Israel, meets with Jehoshaphat, the king of Judah, to discuss battle plans for going to war with Syria. Jehoshaphat insists that before committing to fight, they inquire of God as to his will in the matter. Ahab responds to Jehoshaphat by summoning the prophets and inquiring of them. When the "yes men" prophets all say, "Go up to Ramoth-Gilead, for God has given it into your hand," Jehoshaphat senses something isn't right. He says to Ahab in 1 Kings 22:7, "Is there not here another prophet of the Lord of whom we may inquire?" What made Jehoshaphat ask this? What was he sensing that made him believe that Ahab's prophets couldn't be trusted? The Bible doesn't give us the answers to those questions. However, whatever was behind Jehoshaphat's senses, he clearly knew something wasn't right and understood that Ahab's leadership was going to take him in a dangerous direction.

It is impossible for any person to walk out of deception until they believe deception exists. Truth is the central assumption of all social life. We generally believe that people, government, and religion operate with this shared human value. Deception begins when one party takes advantage of another party's willingness to believe the best about intentions and actions as they hold to this value. When this happens, relationships unknowingly become fraudulent as they are built on a measure of deception. Of course, the deception stemming from a white lie about how your spouse's ugly new haircut looks is far less consequential than a government covering up the truth about going to war with a foreign nation. Nevertheless, both demonstrate the persuasion that deception has in convincing people that a lie is a truth. Moreover, when someone who is deceived believes they are in the right, it is only because they assume they have all the information connected with making their decision. The deceived person never believes their conclusions are a byproduct of bad or false information. This is the reason why deception is so powerful. If a lie can be passed off as truth, an unchallengeable narrative is created. The more people that accept the narrative, the deeper the deception goes, and the more holding power it has over the mind of the masses. Never is this truer than when it comes to an abusive church and the culture surrounding it. The question becomes; if an abusive church or leadership counts on deception as the means to control the way its people think and act, how do the deceived ever get free? The answer is found, in part, in Jehoshaphat's response to Ahab.

When a person finally escapes an abusive leader and the culture that they were a part of, one of the things they always acknowledge is how they knew something was wrong far before they chose to leave. They saw certain things that didn't sit right with them. They would attend ministry meetings and listen to the way people were talked about behind their backs. They saw the way money was being spent or budgets being ignored. They witnessed the inappropriate affections expressed towards the opposite sex.

They saw lies exposed but then covered up by denial. They watched unethical behavior in business dealings with cities and the IRS. They witnessed domineering, abusive interactions with people. They saw the double standards. Through it all, they had the same check in their Spirit as Jehoshaphat had in his. Yet, despite this, they didn't say anything. They chose not to confront the wrong. In fact, they often looked the other way or made excuses for the behavior of the guilty. Why? Was it because they were evil participants? Not usually. Was it because they lacked the fortitude to deal with the fallout if they were the initiators of the confrontation? Maybe in part. In most cases, their silence was not ignorance of the obvious wrong, although we all bear our own responsibility when our silence ought to give way to open expression. On the contrary, it was due to a battle raging inside of them. Their perception of what had been built on lies was being challenged by what they were witnessing. The truth was intersecting with falsehood, which began the slow process of chipping away at the narratives and beliefs they had come to accept. Yet, all the while, there still existed a "Love believes all things" mentality. They were still operating under the social and Biblical value of truth, wanting to extend to their pastor the benefit of the doubt. However, in the end, those that escape all agree. At some point, they crossed a threshold which opened their eyes and didn't allow them to look back. That threshold was when they realized their abuser was a liar. He didn't forget, he didn't misunderstand, he lied! Once the abused saw that one truth, their eyes were opened, their fear disappeared, and they were free!

Those who live through the hurt of being manipulated by people claiming to represent God often think to themselves, "If only I knew then what I know now." This can easily become a person's silent mantra of the heart as they think back to their abusive situations. To be sure, the stroll down memory lane, re-living the past, can be a painful one stirring up a lot of regrets. In some ways, there is a place for this in the healing process because it serves as a reminder of how we could have done things differently. Anytime we can visit the place of self-reflection without it becoming self-condemnation, we become wiser from experience.

One of the greatest desires of those having escaped the grips of spiritual abuse is to share the lessons they learned with those still bound up in it. Thus far, we have covered four cultural norms that are prevalent in abusive church cultures. The problem is when a person doesn't believe they're the victim of spiritual manipulation, telling them about "seduction" won't matter. Explaining the "culture of fear" will have no impact. Warning them about the "culture of lies" and the culture of condemnation will seem useless. The question becomes: "Is there anything that the deceived can look to that might serve as a danger sign and help rattle the cage they find themselves in? Is there anything that can unlock the door to their imprisonment so that with a minimal amount of push on their part, they might find themselves on the path to freedom? Fortunately, there is, and the deceived would do well to pay attention to what comes next.

"There are no perfect churches." If a person has been a Christian long enough, that statement will not shock them. In fact, their personal experiences with people and church leaders will testify to this. Also, "People leave churches." Again, not a shocking revelation if a person has been a Christian for any length of time. People leave churches for a host of reasons. Some move away while others struggle to connect in a relationship. Some people leave churches because they're critical of the music, or the lighting, or the preaching not being funny enough, or the ripped jeans that the worship leader wears on Sundays. Of course, the most common is when someone has been offended. There is no shortage of reasons why people leave churches. Consequently, it is very difficult to judge the health of a church solely on the turnover of its newer congregants or the departure of its faithful supporters. However, there is a certain kind of departure that can be an indicator that something is unhealthy in a church. This departure is when key leaders, such as faithful long-term congregants, ministry leaders, pastors, and elders, exit in a consistent manner with little to no explanation for their departure. Although it is true that even these leaders will move on from time to time, the consistency of their departure in relation to the timing of their departure can be a sign that something is seriously wrong. This was the case at East Lake Church.

East Lake Church was a thriving community of believers. As the church found favor with God and experienced consistent growth over a short period of time, the lead pastor became prideful. He was a loving shepherd on the outside but insecure and emotionally unstable on the inside. If he felt a person crossed him or couldn't be trusted, those people paid the price. He would gossip and slander people by hosting private meetings with their friends, where his gossip and slander was disguised as pastoral care. He controlled his leaders with manipulative stories where he dismantled the reputation of those he despised. He would pull teenagers into his office, telling them lies about people he did not approve of so they would break fellowship with those people. He also caused division between spouses when one wouldn't receive his counsel or suggested that it was unbiblical. In one case he told a man that his wife was in rebellion for not listening to him. He told the man he needed to "control his wife" and "bring her into submission." As his pride swelled and his insecurities surfaced, it became evident to some at his church that something wasn't right. A reputable leader from a para-church organization in the community suddenly quit attending East Lake. Shortly after, one of the worship leaders abruptly left. On the heels of his departure, several faithful congregants suddenly stopped attending. Many of them tried to express their concerns, but there was no Biblical Avenue within the eldership that allowed for it. Not too long after their departure, one of the assistant pastors left. There was no explanation given to the congregation at the time. About six months after his departure, another assistant pastor left. Again, very little was shared and his departure, which was known by the lead pastor months before it happened, was kept from the congregation until the very last minute. The reason was that the lead pastor would have had a hard time explaining why two assistant pastors were leaving within three months of each other. Within a couple of months of his departure, the Bible college director left. Around the same time, a foreign missionary left. Not long after her departure, multiple people (up to 1/3 of the congregation) left. Shortly after them, multiple elders left, all the pastors left, all the staff left, and most ministry leaders left. The pastor's explanation was that everyone was in sin and abandoned their post. Of course, the most naïve embraced the deception in the aftermath and remained under the pastor's leadership, even though the church became a shell of what it once was.

Admittedly, this is an extreme case and not consistent with what most people will experience in their church life. Nonetheless, it underscores an important earmark of an unhealthy church and unhealthy church leadership. Why? Congregants are generally kept from the inner workings and information which flows through the leadership of a church. Ministry leaders to some degree, staff to a greater degree, and pastors and elders to an even greater degree are not. If multiple leaders serving close to a senior leader abruptly depart, what are the chances that all of them lack discernment? What are the chances that all of them are in sin? If each has their own story relating to their own interactions with the same leader, and those interactions justify leaving their shepherding positions, this is something that even the deceived can look at and conclude as Jehoshaphat did, "Something isn't right!" If one pastor or elder leaves a church abruptly, this may mean nothing. It could be the result of a disagreement that couldn't be rectified. There could be a moral failure where the dignity of the departing is being considered in the silence. However, if fifteen leaders leave and ½ the congregation leaves within a four-month span, to ignore that is to willingly chain yourself next to the two remaining prisoners in Plato's cave. To ignore that means to insist on living in the dark, where deception is a person's only reality.

In James 3:18, we're told, "The fruit of righteousness is sown in peace by those that make peace." In other words, peacemakers sow peace which produces the fruit of righteousness. Therefore, a person cannot lay claim to righteous behavior or righteous standing if they are not sowing peace! This is something even the deceived can look for. If an abusive leader is as righteous as he usually contends to be, then look around him for the peace that justifies his claim to righteous standing. Look at the people he interacts with. Is there peace in his marriage or is there war and ruin? Is there peace in his home with those he leads, or is there war and ruin? Does he seek out those who he knows he's at odds with to reconcile the relationship, or does he claim righteousness with no pursuit of sowing peace? What about the people he surrounds himself with? His staff? The hopelessly devoted congregant that has both sides of the story as told by one side? Are they at peace with people in their life in such a way that justifies their claim of righteous standing? Are they separated or at war with their siblings, their daughters, their relatives, and others? In the name of "righteousness," have they separated from those people that have been maligned by their leader's slander? The Bible knows of no such righteousness without the pursuit of peace with others. Any proclamation to the contrary is simply the denial of God's word. To worship in a religious culture which regularly shuns, and isolates people made in the image of God, is one of the greatest signs that a person's deception is rooted in the adoration of sinful man and not the worship of the Prince of Peace!

To escape the grips of an abusive church, a person must pay attention! They must pay attention to the inconsistencies around them. They must pay attention to the narratives that say one thing in November but something different in February. A person must be willing to recognize that November wasn't a, "misunderstanding." February was a lie! Like Jehoshaphat, they must pay attention to the Spirit inside of them that is saying, "Something is off." They cannot be afraid of where the Spirit may lead them! Naturally, they temper all things with grace and mercy for others just as they want the same. However, they cannot be naïve when all the signs are pointing to the obvious, nor can they allow the abuser to redefine the obvious. To escape the grip of spiritual abuse, the abused need to see their abuser for who they are, a misrepresentation of God seeking to draw men after themselves! Perhaps they're a wolf in sheep's clothing or just an extremely deceived and carnal believer. Regardless, the abused need to realize that they don't owe their abuser anything! Their devotion is to God, and their call is to put themselves under leaders who understand this. To escape, they must realize they have the right to reject those who would lead them with a shepherd's staff while injecting them with serpent's venom. To escape the grip of spiritual abuse, a person cannot be afraid of what the manipulator can do to them or how he might threaten them. Indeed, they must be able to say to their abuser as Jesus to Pilate when he was threatened, "You have no authority over me other than what's been given to you." Finally, to escape the abuse, the abused must be willing to leave, and if necessary, by themselves!

When a person chooses to get away from the abusive control of an unhealthy pastor or leader, it can be a lonely place. A natural distrust for people can easily develop, not to mention distrust for the church. An isolation mentality can even form, making the idea of Christian fellowship repulsive. This explains why many people want nothing to do with the church in the immediate aftermath of their abusive experience. Their trust has been broken. Their vulnerability has been taken advantage of. Their hurt is deep. They often have a difficult time reading the Bible because all they hear is their abuser's voice quoting the scriptures. It's as if their abuse has never stopped. They have a hard time separating their abuser's hypocritical explanation of scripture from the purity and holiness of its truths. For some people, this one fact alone makes healing seem like it's impossible. After all, if God's word is what heals the soul, but their abuser's misuse of God's Word is what damaged it, how can they trust the thing they see as responsible for the damage? This emphasizes the need for fellowship with others who have experienced the same type of trauma.

The Apostle Paul said, in 2 Corinthians 1:4, that "God comforts us in our tribulation, that we may be able to comfort those who are in any trouble, with the same comfort with which we ourselves were comforted." As mentioned in the previous chapter, when a person is in the process of discovering an unhealthy church, they are often made to feel crazy by their abuser. Since the culture won't allow a person to discuss their perceptions with anyone other than their abuser without the fear of being branded "a gossip," they are left unaware of anyone else who might be experiencing the same. We'll discuss this more in the next chapter on healing from the abuse. However, when a person needs to escape the abuse, the experiences of those who have gone before them can be encouraging and helpful. For this reason, a person considering leaving a spiritually toxic environment should seek out those who they know have gone before them. There are stories that haven't been told that will serve as validation for the "Jehoshaphat sense" the abused is experiencing within. This type of collaboration, though branded by the abuser as "unhealthy gossip," isn't gossip at all. People are allowed to gather information if they're trying to determine truth for protection against deception! Proverbs 18 calls such pursuit of information—"wise."

People that are leaving spiritually manipulative situations must be willing to walk away and walk alone if they're going to escape the grip of the abuse. There is often a huge cost associated with the decision to leave. The abused should expect to see some of their closest relationships severed. This might include being cut off by their own family if their family chooses to remain in what they are choosing to leave behind. It's not that the severing of such family relationships is the choice of the abused, to the contrary. However, the people remaining in the cultic culture will have no choice but to distance themselves from any naysayers if they wish to maintain good standing and show themselves to be loyal followers of their leaders. Also, the escapee must be willing to give up their reputation, knowing that lies will be told about them. They will likely have to walk away from several friendships because isolation will be the abuser's response to their "abandonment of the faith." They will have to suffer the frustration of having their abuser campaign against their character. This campaign may extend to their workplace, their school, and even their next house of worship. Many stories have been told of abusive leaders contacting former congregants' new churches to "tip off" the leadership of the "harmfulness" of the people that escaped their deception. Though there may be extreme situations where this is appropriate, in most cases, it only serves as further evidence of the narcissistic nature behind the abuser's leadership style.

The "campaigning" against people's character can venture into borderless expressions of evil. Meaning when the abuser is consumed with his evil desire to control people and manipulate information, there are no limits to what he will do. I know of a situation where a senior pastor went after a teenage congregant by isolating her from her friends who attended his church. They were pulled into private meetings and discouraged from associating with her. Many of those relationships ended as a result and the teenager was crushed. This desperation always seems to lead to an "abuse by proxy." This means that the abuser goes beyond the cultic culture he's established in his church and uses other loyal followers to administer his abuse to those he cannot control. The reason for this is twofold. First, because there is an insatiable desire to make the uncompliant look as bad as possible in the eyes of others. This is connected to a convoluted way of thinking that tells him if people see the sinfulness of his opposition, they will naturally conclude that he is the righteous one in the dispute. The abuser loves the "victim" status this grants him in the eyes of others. This is the altar the abuser worships at. It's all about self. The abuser finds his identity in the perception of being just and holy, not in the reality of it!

Secondly, by using others to propagate his evil, he protects himself if accusations arise of wrongdoing. Since this "abuse by proxy" is technically carried out by others, the abuser can claim innocence if it turns out that his abuse is exposed. This "abuse by proxy" has many faces and can be a little hard to detect at first. The reason is that the abuser uses the relationships closest to the ones he's abusing. The abused are usually unsuspecting at the beginning because the perpetrators are their best friends, parents, and sons and daughters. Their assault comes at the hands of their family and friends gathering information through dinners, recordings, and "innocent" coffee meetings. There is a certain kind of stealth in this approach as the victim never suspects that through their valued relationships, their abuser is propagating betrayal. When the abused eventually find out, the betrayal leaves the relationship in shambles. This type of insanity may last for a short season before relationships are restored. However, it may also last the rest of a person's life. Also, the awkwardness of public run-ins with those who remain in the cult will be felt in the grocery store, at the restaurant, at the gym, and at community events. There will also be a degree of shame that will be experienced as the abused realizes how they treated others before escaping their abuser.

Escaping abuse is a process and because it is, there are many contributing factors to someone getting free. A person's own mental instability should not be ignored. When someone is considering leaving their church for reasons of domineering leadership, their mental state will likely reflect that of a young child missing their ADHD medication. When under the bondage of abuse, there's a certain mental strain that is the antithesis of the peace one would expect to find in following Christ. Because of the abusive leader's lying, chaotic ways, he makes everyone around him share in his misery. Though he may be accustomed to ordering his life in such chaos, most people are not. Consequently, ministry and service become a burden. There's confusion around every corner. There is also a general oppression and sometimes depression not normally felt. This tends to envelop the victim's church experience leaving them with a desire to be away from church more than being a part of it. If a person thinks their church is abusive, their mental instability should be considered as a viable contributor to their decision to leave.

When freedom from spiritual tyranny is experienced, a person finds a newfound love for Jesus Christ. Grace is given a makeover from the dark gothic look it had under their abuser. Scripture comes to life outside the prison cell of manipulation as a person discovers the beauty of what the Bible says about Godly leadership and selfless shepherding. When free, a person finds the acceptance of Christ to be far more motivating than the acceptance of their irrelevant abuser.

Chapter 6

Healing From the Abuse

> ***"But for you who fear my name, the Sun of Righteousness will rise with healing in its wings. And you will go free, leaping with joy..."***
> *– Malachi 4:2*

As parents, we all have one or two memories of our kids when they were younger, sustaining that injury that made us say, "Oh no, this isn't good!" For me, it was when my son was about three years old and decided to pull each of his five dresser drawers out to use as a ladder. He was trying to change the DVD on the television that was on top of his dresser. I was in the kitchen when I heard the loud crash. I ran into his room to see the dresser and television lying on top of him. As I picked the dresser up, all I could see was blood all over his face. His forehead had been cut open by the weight of the oak dresser and television. Moments later, we were in the car headed to the emergency room, where he received several stitches to close the cut. Today there is only a tiny scar to serve as a reminder of what was so traumatic to him at the time.

Whenever a person sustains a cut, within seconds of the injury, their blood begins to clot. These clots form what we know as a scab. The clot contains fibrin, a protein which helps the healing process of the wound. Over time, new tissue is built as the scab dissipates and eventually disappears, leaving only the scar as a reminder of the injury. Most scars become less noticeable with time as the wound heals. However, despite the healing, the damaged skin never really reaches 100% of its strength, and depending on the severity of the wound, some scars never completely vanish.

If our bodies are naturally designed by God to recover from trauma, then the same can be said about our heart and mind. When a person incurs a gash on their forehead, the evidence of the injury is indicated by the presence of blood. The more blood that flows from the wound, the more severe the wound usually is. The more severe the wound is, the longer it takes to heal. Therefore, the most essential part of treating any injury where blood is flowing is to stop the bleeding. Healing cannot begin if there is a constant flow of blood!

As we illuded to in the last chapter, if a person finds themselves in a church where the spiritual oversight is abusive, eventually, they will have to leave. They cannot find healing for their soul in the place that is causing the damage. This may seem like a "no brainer", but some choose a different route. Thinking they can inspire change, well-meaning people often stay in abusive situations longer than they should. Their intentions are usually good, but the damage that is done to their heart and mind while they wait in the hope for an outcome that never transpires cannot be understated. They must "stop the bleeding" if they are to heal. Meaning they must put distance between themself and their abuser. It is the only way that their heart can "scab up" and their recovery process can begin. Therefore, the two foundational parts of healing from spiritual abuse are distance and time.

The dictionary definition of "distance" is "The amount of space between two things or people." In the context of our usage of the word, it means to be separated from the thing or person that is causing hurt. No person has the right to damage the spiritual well-being of another. God has not granted such authority to any man. Heavy-handed leadership is forbidden in the New Testament, as is treating God's people harshly to fulfill a carnal desire for recognition, authority, or position. It is expected that mature leaders understand this and order their lives with great humility. However, the final say as to what an abusive person is allowed to do to his victim lies with the victim, not the abuser! The abuser may think he gets the last word with his slanderous campaign to dismantle the reputation of the one he abuses, but that's only self-illusion. The truth is that his victim gets the last word! The abused take back all of the control they surrendered the minute they leave their abuser! They render the voice, influence, and opinions of their abuser to be irrelevant when they show him their back. They immediately return to the place of equality with the one they were led to believe held superiority. Their weakness is replaced with strength. Their dependency upon their abuser is replaced with a restored confidence and faith in God's sovereignty. With every step away from their abuser, the distance serves as a protection from future assault. In some cases, the abuse can be so severe that people have no choice but to move to different cities, counties, and even states. Such responses are often necessary, so healing can take place without interference coming from the abuser. Some situations require blocking the perpetrator from social media accounts to stop the online stocking and spying on thread conversations. In the most extreme cases, "No Contact" orders are sought by pursuing legal avenues against the abuser. The more distance that a person can create between them and the one who hurts them, the more likely a full recovery can take place. The abused must be aware that there is always the danger of continuing to hurt if there are connection points that can be established between them and their abuser. The abuser will pursue, with vigor, any relational door that gives him access to continue his assault on his victim. Therefore, the distance that needs to be created in the most extreme cases is one of complete and total severing. This may be for a season until the abused regains their emotional stability and is able to put immovable boundaries in place that will be honored by others. However, the severing may also be permanent. The decision ultimately rests with the abused and how comfortable they are with their perpetrator's repentance and assurance that the abusive behavior is a thing of the past.

It's important that when the abused are forced into a corner and the only way out is severing relationships, they aren't made to feel guilty by those around them. They need to always keep in mind that they are responding to their abuser. The abused should be careful never to judge themselves for what others have done to them! This is important because when the abused finally take back control and separate themselves from the one who hurt them, the abuser will play the victim. The abuser will gather support and sympathy from those who still stay close to him. In what becomes a twisted turn of events, he will assume the role of the abused. It won't be long before his victim is being accused of being harsh and over-reactive in their response to sever ties. This, of course, is the ultimate form of gaslighting and the abused should not be moved by this deception.

Forgiveness is essential for those who have been spiritually abused by a church or its leaders. In fact, forgiving those who have hurt us in life may be one of the greatest demonstrations of our understanding, for our own need to be forgiven by God. To be sure, the New Testament is full of instructions to forgive others of the debt we feel they owe us. Luke 6:37 says, "Forgive, and you will be forgiven." Luke 17:3 tells us that if someone repents of a sin committed against us, we are to forgive them. Finally, Matthew 18:35 says that when a Christian forgives, he must forgive "from the heart." What exactly does it mean to "forgive from the heart?" Some have suggested that it means a person simply forgets the offense ever took place. Some go as far as to say that unless we forgive to the point of forgetting, then we haven't truly forgiven. Others say that you'll know a person has chosen to forgive when they've been reconciled with the one who hurt them. Is this Biblical forgiveness? Do the victims of other people's sins simply erase the experience from their memory? Of course not. One of the ways we learn and apply wisdom is to live it through our experiences—the good and the bad. Victims of abuse can recognize their forgiveness from the heart when they imagine their abuser's apology and their response is, "I forgive you." On the other hand, if the abused think of their response and it's: "No, I don't accept your apology and I hope an asteroid lands on your head while you are eating lunch today," then they are probably closer to bitterness than forgiveness. Nonetheless, when a person is abused by what is supposed to be the safest place on earth—God's church, we should never assume that triggering reminders, which provoke emotional responses, are necessarily signs of unforgiveness. Most of the time, this is simply a part of the normal grieving process that helps a person heal. There are stages of grief that a person must go through on their way to recovery. If during one of those stages, a line is crossed in the victim's heart, God is able to cover their sin. He can give grace and mercy to the abused as they move from grief towards wholeness. This, of course, happens over time, which leads us to the second foundation of healing from spiritual abuse.

Time is as essential to healing the hurt heart as it is to the open wound. There are important aspects to healing from spiritual abuse that can only happen over time. Although it is true that some people may experience wholeness faster than others, everyone affected by abuse needs time to heal. There is an incredible loss associated with spiritual abuse. Friendships are often never the same, some are completely ruined. Families are fractured, some beyond repair. A person's faith in God is often shaken and some turn their back for good. There is also the dark shadow that is cast over the reputation of the local church, as outsiders and insiders are given occasion to smear the good work of the Holy Spirit. However, as great a loss as there may be, there is also a great opportunity for personal growth in the healing process.

As was mentioned before, fellowship with believers who have gone through similar trauma is helpful. However, more helpful is when the abused can connect with other victims of the same perpetrator from the same abusive church. This helps because when two victims of the same abuser can see how they were both deceived, lies are brought to light. A person's psyche often feels a sense of vindication and return to sanity, knowing that they weren't alone in their perception of the abuse. The victims also realize their part in hurting others while they were under the deception of the abuser. It can be a humiliating time for the victim because it brings to the surface their part in helping establish and preserve the abusive culture that eventually turned on them. What usually follows is a plethora of calls, coffee dates, and lunch appointments with former congregants, apologizing for the hurt they caused. This is necessary because it begins the restoration of relationships damaged by the abuse. It's understandable that participating in hurting others is an embarrassment, but to heal properly a person needs to own their contribution to the whole of the abuse. For someone to ignore this because they feel ashamed by the damage they've caused to others only continues the division that the abuser initiated. The simple words, "I'm sorry, I was wrong for what I did," are powerful first steps to repairing the damage caused by the abuser.

Also, the restoration of relationships sends a message to the abuser. It says that despite all the efforts to control people by sowing discord in their relationships, it failed! There is nothing quite as sweet as when friends are reconciled, and their common abuser is left to reflect on his failed efforts to divide the body of Christ.

It's been said, "Time heals all wounds." I disagree. Time isn't a miracle worker, Jesus is. The truth is Jesus heals all wounds over time, or at least most wounds. However, there are things we contribute to our own healing. One of those things is Biblical accountability and mentorship. Every Christian should have other Christians in their life that provide accountability and mentorship. Never is this more important than when a person is recovering from spiritual abuse. A lot of damage happens to a person's thought process when they've been manipulated. When manipulation is presented as "spiritual care," even greater damage takes place. Biblical mentorship and accountability help restore right thinking. Therefore, it is essential that those wanting to heal from spiritual abuse find mature, healthy believers to walk with them through the process. This isn't to say that the abused are incapable of proper thinking in all matters pertaining to life. However, the emotional trauma of this type of abuse can skew a person's spiritual outlook on life. There is often anger and rage following the escape from spiritually abusive situations. Having a mentor help walk the victim through the anger, processing it through scripture, is essential to healing. Also, victims of spiritual abuse often want nothing to do with God once they walk away from their abuser. Having a Christian mentor helps keep the victim's emotions in check, which may prevent them from making decisions that might affect their eternity.

Additionally, in extreme cases of abuse, professional counseling, along with Biblical mentorship, may be necessary. The brain is an organ and there are physiological ramifications of spiritual abuse. Professional Christian counseling can help the abused get healthy.

Another thing that may be helpful in the healing process is for the victim to confront their abuser. I say, "Maybe," because there are some cases where it could backfire and give another opportunity for abuse to occur. However, some forms of communication can serve as closure for the victim. Often, letters or emails can be safe avenues for such confrontation. The reason is that there can be no interruption as there often is in a personal conversation. The abuser has no choice but to "listen" to his victim if he reads their letter or email. Additionally, when something is written down, lies can be dispelled, whereas in personal conversations, it's easy to deny things were said. There is a warning if a person chooses this path to communicate. The victim should by no means open a dialogue with their abuser! This will only give another opportunity for the abuser to gaslight and confuse his victim. If a person chooses this avenue to confront their abuser, their letter or email should be prefaced with something that says, "I will not be reading any response you might send, as this is not an invitation to further conversation." Of course, the narcists will not abide by any guidelines for communication, particularly those that don't give him the last word. Therefore, the victim will have to delete his response the moment he sends it without reading it. This will ensure that the recovery process isn't interrupted by further manipulation from the abuser. If the victim does choose to meet their abuser in person, they should seriously consider bringing someone else with them, as well as recording the conversation. The additional person will serve as a witness to what is said, making it more difficult to misconstrue when others are told about the meeting. Also, the recording will do the same. The victim should be upfront with their intention to record the conversation by telling their abuser they do not believe them to be an honest person. Therefore, for their own protection, they are recording the conversation. Since spiritually abusive leaders hate being accountable to truth, they will likely be uncomfortable at this suggestion and not want to talk.

The aftermath of escaping spiritual abuse can be mentally exhausting. It can put strains on marriages and friendships. One of the fallouts is often a detachment from personal devotion with God. Picking up the Bible, for some, becomes difficult. One victim said, "I don't want to read the Bible because every time I do, I hear my abuser's voice quoting the scripture." A pastor who escaped an abusive church also said, "There are certain verses I don't even want to read anymore because of how often they were quoted in trying to control me." This might be where the greatest damage is done to a person. The Bible is God's Word for a broken world. It's the one place where the believer is supposed to be able to turn to find rest for their souls. It's supposed to provide direction to the confused and encouragement to the disappointed. It also is supposed to mend the broken heart and give back hope to the hopeless.

Therefore, in the aftermath of spiritual abuse, healing requires that the victim re-establish the prominence of God's Word in their life. They must remember their abuser used something that wasn't theirs in a way that God never gave permission to be used. The victim must make the separation in their mind that it was not God who used his word to bring hurt, it was the sinful abuser who did! The trustworthiness of scripture pertaining to the preservation of mental stability through its instructions and encouragement must be put back in the place from where the abuser knocked it off. Simply put, healing will require submission to God's Word in all things. The abuse is unfortunate and horrific, but it cannot be used as an excuse to avoid the truth of scripture for a person's healing. May it not be said that the abuser's ungodly conduct was all that was needed to expose the victim's shallow commitment to God and his Word! Healing from spiritual abuse will require some resilience, it will also produce it. Those healing need to return to the mind that was stolen from them. That is, God is the source of our worship, not men! Men will usually disappoint us and will often misrepresent the heart of God. However, God will always have our best interest in mind as it relates to his will and plan for our life.

Chapter 7

A Letter to the Abused

Dear Friend,

If you're reading this book, you are likely in one of three positions. First, you are still a part of an abusive church and do not see the damage being done to you or the damage you are doing to others. Secondly, you still attend an abusive church, but you see that something isn't right and you're deeply concerned. Lastly, you have left an abusive church and you are on the road to recovering from your hurt. Also, in this last group are those who have left and found healing. I would like to address each of these three groups.

To begin with, to those of you still under the abusive hand of your church leaders, but you don't see it, be careful. The longer you remain "Believing the Best," the more hurt you will be responsible for. The fear of the Lord ought to be a continual motivator for you to be sure that your allegiance is to Christ and not a man, to the truth and not a lie. Therefore, I would encourage you to revisit the words of Jesus in Matthew 24:4 when he says;

"See to it that no one deceives you."

Every person is responsible for their own choices in what information they allow to persuade them. If your leadership spiritually abuses people, you will not perceive it as abuse!

Your loyalty to the man, your position, your reputation, and the relationships you have in the church will not allow you to. The fear of losing any of those will disguise itself as righteous and holy behavior in your decisions. To be sure, until the abuse turns on you, you will not want to recognize it. The consideration that you might be enabling an abuser might cross your mind from time to time. However, the fear of what the cost might be if you responded to those considerations will keep you shackled, so allow me to be blunt. Scripture commands that to follow Christ as one of his disciples, you must be willing to give up everything mentioned above! In Luke 14:26-33, Jesus made this clear. He said:

> *"If anyone comes to me and does not hate his own father and mother and wife and children and brothers and sisters, yes, and even his own life, he cannot be my disciple... so therefore, any one of you who does not renounce all that he has, cannot be my disciple."*

In these passages, Jesus uses the closest relationships given to mankind as an example of what the cost will be if a person chooses to be a faithful disciple. Therefore, included in this list must also be every relationship on earth that is inferior to those mentioned. This means that to be Christ's disciple, you must not honor an abusive church leader's relationship more than your relationship with God! Furthermore, there must not be anything that the abuser holds that he can use as collateral to ensure your loyalty. This would include the threat of you being isolated from friends and family. To fear the loss of any relationship that the abuser might directly or indirectly threaten you with and allow it to keep you from doing what is right is idolatry! It means you're being mastered by fear and not faith. What exactly are you afraid of? Do you understand that your abuser has convinced you that he holds spiritual authority over you that God never gave him? You might be saying to yourself, "Hold on! Hebrews 13:17 tells me to submit to my church leaders. In fact, that's my pastor's favorite verse." As I mentioned earlier in the book, read the entirety of the passages preceding it. I am not advocating for a rogue lifestyle in the church that usurps the Biblical oversight of a shepherd. However, submission to that oversight has some very clear conditions attached to it. Hebrews 13:17 must be read with first consideration being given to Hebrews 13:7, which says:

> *"Remember those who rule over you, who have spoken the word of God to you, whose faith follow, considering the outcome of their conduct."*

Notice the submission to leadership in the church is not a blind acceptance of anything they say or do. It's contingent upon their faith and the outcome of their conduct. If their conduct betrays scripture, then to be told that you are not submitting when you challenge the holiness of their conduct is for them to place themselves above the protective custody that scripture ensures to the faithful! Why do you allow this? Why are you so quick to reject any information that might be contrary to your leader's narrative? Ask yourself this question: "Do I currently have strife in my relationships with others that is due to information I've received from my pastor or leaders?" If your answer to that question is "Yes," then ask yourself another question, "Have I gone to the people that I'm at odds with, that I'm gossiping and slandering, and asked them if the information I have is correct?" If your answer is anything other than "Yes," then you are sinning against God to fear a man! If your excuse is that your pastor or leader will find out and deem you to be unloyal or in sin, then you have just confirmed that your spiritual authority is abusive and controlling! Any church leader or pastor that would make you feel fearful for obeying scripture as you seek peace with others does not represent God!

Additionally, when Jesus says that a person must be willing to renounce "All that he has, or he cannot be my disciple," he goes beyond relationship. Here, Jesus ventures into what a man possesses. This could refer to many things. What is it that you possess that your abusive leader uses as your chains? Is it your position? If you're truly called by God, couldn't you find another position? Is it your title? Do you find your identity by others calling you "Rabbi (Matthew 23:7)? Maybe it's your reputation or ministry? If Jesus made himself of no reputation (Phil 2:7), are you not willing to sacrifice yours? Maybe you think he holds the future to your ministry aspirations? So, now it's a man and not God who "brings down one and exalts another (Psalm 75:7)?" Is it an income he uses to shackle you? Can he affect your professional life? Your job? With all due respect, is this how cheap your loyalty to God has become? Will you sell out to a fabricated view that your abusive leader has more authority over you than he really does? You were not created by God to live in this type of controlling fear! I can assure you that your abuser only has the control you are willing to give him through the fear you render to him! So, my plea is that you would open your eyes to the reality around you, not to what your abuser says it is. You know that two plus two equals four. You are too smart to be told that it equals five! If the faithful Christians around you were Godly in the eyes of your abuser while they were loyal to him, but suddenly they were in sin when they left his leadership, is this not something for you to consider? Why are you willing to accept harmful narratives and sinful accusations against people you've always known to love the Lord? Why aren't you willing to be in a relationship with the people your leadership is at odds with? Did they offend you? Is it possible you're being manipulated, thinking loyalty to God is expressed by taking up the offense of your abusive leader? You are allowed to think for yourself! You are called to be at peace with all people as much as it depends on you (Romans 12:18). If being at peace with people and in a relationship with those who have done you no wrong is discouraged by your leaders, then consider God's feelings on the matter. Proverbs 6:16-19 says:

> *There are six things that the LORD hates,*
> *seven that are an abomination to him:*
> *haughty eyes, a lying tongue,*
> *and hands that shed innocent blood,*
> *a heart that devises wicked plans,*
> *feet that make haste to run to evil,*

> *a false witness who breathes out lies,*
> *and one who sows discord among brothers.*

Notice v.16 says the seventh thing mentioned is "an abomination" to the Lord. The seventh thing mentioned is "one who sows discord among the brethren." The picture is of a farmer throwing out seeds to grow a crop. In this case, the seed is division, and the soil is the people's minds and hearts. When the seeds of division are sown amongst the people through gossiping and slandering, the crop it yields is separation and hatred. Justify your decision to separate from the people who have done you no wrong and with whom you have never spoken. Who authors such a behavior, God? Certainly not! My friend, I urge you to embrace the Spirit's prodding within you when you sense something isn't right. God gave that to you for your protection! If you choose to fear the abuser and live within the culture he has built while ignoring all the evidence around you, then you will be partly responsible for damaging people's souls! If that does not move you to consider investigating what you have embraced, then my prayer is that the Lord would open your eyes to the deception you refuse to protect yourself against.

Secondly, to the one still a part of the abuse, but you see it and have a great concern as you're considering your next steps. Oh, how I want to encourage you with this. You are not crazy! I'm sure that in your consideration of what's next, you are wondering if your perception of things is right. Accompanying your concern is no doubt a certain amount of confusion. You are still close to a lot of the people who don't see what you see. They're your friends, family members, and co-workers. You've respected their opinions in the past and, in many ways, still do. Their inability to see what you see has frustrated you and even serves as a temptation for you to ignore what you now know to be true. You've likely had several confrontations with the abusive leaders, and you're starting to feel the pinch of isolation. Your friends are a little more standoffish than usual and you might have been approached by several people encouraging you to repent and submit to your abuser. It's also possible that you've been in meetings where your abuser has tried to convince you to believe things about yourself that aren't true. In some ways, you almost feel like you're prosecuting yourself for crimes you didn't commit. You've sat through conversations where your words have been twisted and weaponized to assault your character. You've been told by your abuser that you've said things that were never said, and when you tried to hold your abuser accountable to truth, he rearranged history, and past conversations magically disappeared. Besides this, you go to sleep thinking about your abuse and you wake up with it being first on your mind.

Also, by this time, you have likely been removed from serving in the church, or have been given reduced responsibilities, or you're enjoying the solitude of a "break" or "sabbatical" so you can reflect and consider your "rebellious heart." You are also basking in the joy of Sunday messages that are "divinely inspired" to publicly address the very "rebellion" you are being accused of in private. So, as you consider your next steps, allow me to encourage you with this one, leave! Things will not improve unless you capitulate to the abuser. If your convictions are such that you cannot submit to the abusive leadership's demands, and there is no evidence that things will change, then your choice is simple, just leave. Isn't it worth exchanging the heartache and the insanity that comes from the abuse for the peace and serenity that comes from being in the presence of God? Your identity is not found in the church you attend, it's found in the God who died for your sins! Here is a liberating thought: "You get to choose who shepherds you!" You get to vote with your feet as to who invests in your spiritual walk! If you're in a relationship with God, and your motivation for leaving is to preserve that relationship, then be assured that the Lord will walk out with you. Jesus said he would never leave you nor forsake you. He didn't say that this promise is contingent upon you being in a certain church. Sure, if you leave the side of your abuser, you'll be told that "You're abandoning your post," or "Putting your hand to the plow and looking back," or even "Leaving the Savior" altogether. Who cares, your abuser's assessments are irrelevant!

Here is what I know—you will be okay. The fears that Satan designs in our minds are meant to keep us in bondage. He wants the chaos that is causing you anxiety to continue. So, when you really believe that God will come to your rescue and be your advocate, when you really believe that "no weapon formed against you will stand," then take your step of faith! I have personally seen in my own life that God gives increasing clarity once you step out and distance yourself from your abuser—situations become clearer. The fog that saturates your thought life dissipates and you can think with the absence of confusion. Your experience creates a sensitivity towards people and you actually treat them the way God designed.

I know you have a fear that people will walk away from you. You're afraid that valued relationships will end. The truth is, that very well may happen. However, I want to encourage you with something I have witnessed personally, God loves to restore! There was a situation I was a part of where many friends and family members were divided because of an abusive leader. A lot of investment through dark conversations, persuasive lies and slander, took place behind closed doors. People's reputations were ruined in the eyes of their families and friends. Holidays missed the peace that usually accompanied them because of division and strife among siblings, parents, and children. However, as truth prevailed and the Spirit of God moved, people's eyes were opened! Reconciliation took place. Sure, some relationships ended, but some made it through, and many became stronger. The abuser was left with the reality that in all of his assault on the Bride of Christ, God protected her, delivered her, and brought reconciliation among her! This is what happens when you get away from the source of your abuse.

What are you waiting for? Scripture promises you will not be alone. God will lead you to a healthy church where people will have compassion on your situation. You are worth more than the treatment you've been exposed to. Christianity is never to be about the church or leadership controlling you but rather serving you! This is what Jesus meant when he spoke to his followers in Matthew 20:25:

> *"You know that the rulers in this world lord over their people, and officials flaunt their authority over those under them, but among*

you it will be different. Whoever wants to be a leader among you, must be your servant."

When Ronald Reagan was running for president, at the end of one of his debates, he looked into the camera and asked the American people this, "Ask yourself a question, are you better off today than you were four years ago?" His intention behind the question was obvious, he wanted to know if people believed their lives were going in the right direction. If their answer was "No," his response was, "Then make a change in your leadership." I would ask those of you that are witnessing abuse on the part of your leaders, "Do you feel your shepherds are going in the right direction? Do you see love prevailing and covering the sinner's faults? Do you see honesty and not deception? Do you hear the best about people being spoken to in private? If your answer to these questions is "No," then make a change in your leadership! Leave the abuse immediately!

Finally, to those who have left and are in the process of healing—Praise God! I am inspired by your boldness to walk away from the abuse that takes place in the "Name of God." The Lord opened your eyes. I'm not sure what your situation took for that to happen, but I rejoice that it did happen! You are likely going through several phases of grief. Depending on where you're at when you read this will determine your response to what I share with you. Let me start by saying you are not ignorant, stupid, or undiscerning because you were captivated by your abuser's charm and deceit. Stop kicking yourself and wishing you could have a "do-over" with the information you now have. The abuse was evil and authored by the deceiver, who is the serpent. He has been at this for a long time and knows every person's make-up. All of us have been victims of his deception at some point in our lives. Do not put yourself under the weight of a condemnation that is not given by God. You are also probably feeling vulnerable in the aftermath of your spiritual abuse. Consequently, you are struggling with even wanting to trust a church or church leadership again. You might even be contemplating leaving the church altogether. I want to encourage you to hold off on that decision. You have been deceived by a man or group of men claiming to represent God. It's understandable for you to connect their ungodly actions with the God they claim to represent. It's also understandable that you want to hold the whole of the church responsible for your hurt. I get it. However, you need to remember that church leaders are sinners like everyone else. They can lie and manipulate while using their revered position to gain credibility in the eyes of those they deceive. Few things are more sinister. However, the only one that really represents God is Jesus!

He is the sinless one. He alone leads with your best interest in mind. He never thinks of his own life above yours. So, what should be your response now that you're out from underneath the abuse having this uncertainty about the goodness of God? Seek the person of Jesus! Go back and familiarize yourself with how he treated every type of person. How did he treat the Woman caught in adultery in John 8? What was his response to James and John in Luke 9:54 when they wanted to call fire down from heaven to destroy the Samaritan villages that wouldn't submit to Jesus? How did he treat the tax collectors and sinners when he ate with them in Matthew 9:10? What about his scathing indictment of the religious leaders in Matthew 23? You see, you must go back to Jesus and allow him to represent himself! This is the only thing that will erase the false impression of Christ left behind by your abuser. The good shepherd did not hurt you, the bad shepherd did!

As I mentioned in the last chapter, the most important thing for you right now is to find Christian fellowship with people whose faith you can respect. Look for a couple of people that will walk with you and speak the truth to you. Your hurt heart may not be ready for corporate gathering in a new church, but you need mature Christians that can help keep your abuse in perspective and encourage you as you make your way back to fellowship. You will have rough days where anger or shame may reign, but "God's mercies are new every morning!" Keep going! Try not to blame every pastor you encounter for the sins of the one who did you wrong. No person can live in the shadows of another sinner's failures. There are many faithful leaders that would count it a joy to invest in your spiritual well-being. Therefore, cut off any communication with your abuser if it seems that there is continuing manipulation that is preventing you from healing. Finally, give yourself some grace! You will have a host of emotions that express themselves as you heal. Some of these emotions will be sinful. Ask the Lord for forgiveness and move on! God is able to handle the sin stemming from the backlash of your abuse.

Lastly, to those who have escaped and experienced healing, share your story! Help others! Let them know what abuse looks like. Comfort them with the same comfort you were given (2 Corinthians 1:4). Blow the trumpet to warn people of the danger you see approaching (Ezekiel 33:1-6). And Encourage them to remain in the faith!

Agape,

Steve

Chapter 8

A Letter to the Abuser

To The Abuser,

By now, there are one of two reactions running through your mind. The first is nothing, no reaction at all. The reason there's nothing is because you don't think yourself to be a spiritually abusive leader. Your conscience has been seared. This is common amongst your type, and I'll address it in a moment. The second possible reaction is conviction. You have deep conviction because you know you've hurt people and ruled with an iron fist instead of a shepherd's staff. I'd like to address the latter before the former.

To the one who's feeling conviction because of the way you've treated those put under your care—repent. Stop doing what you're doing and go the other direction. I realize the difficulty in this because it may be all you know. If you were brought up under an abusive leader within an abusive culture, you are just repeating the cycle out of ignorance, not realizing there is a better way, a Godly way. You have likely had domineering leaders over you in the past and you've come to view aggressive, heavy-handedness as a virtue. You've watched this style of leadership command the respect of people, not realizing it was fear that was operating instead. In some twisted way, your past has taught you that the pastorate is a type of throne that one ascends to by bowing to the tyrant before them. Now that it's your turn to "rule," you lead the same way and expect the same submission. Of course, you and those before you would refer to this style as "strong leadership," but is it really? Jesus was a strong leader, but he never demeaned or belittled the people he was serving. Jesus was more worthy than any human being in history to receive glory while on earth, certainly far more worthy than you. Yet, we're told in Philippians 2:7 that "He emptied himself, taking on the form of a servant." Although you would never admit to not being a servant-leader since that would be unbiblical and you've likely counseled others on the matter, the truth is your style of leadership is all about you. Somewhere along the road, you came to believe that embarrassing people in the office or on the stage before service was okay. Your hungry ego needs recognition from others to validate your authority and calling from God, even if that authority is used to hurt people. This is not the heart of the Lord!

Convictions are puzzling things. Their presence in a person's life is often viewed as the "end all." What do I mean? People tend to think that if they feel bad about something, those convictions are tantamount to repentance. Consequently, this type of "repentance" begins with a feeling and ends with a feeling and has no tangible evidence of its existence. What this means practically is that a person can do something or say something that hurts another, and if they feel bad, it ends there. However, this is not repentance. Repentance is an action, conviction is not. Conviction may be the doorway that repentance walks through since no person is going to repent of something they don't believe they've done wrong, but repentance can be seen by others. So, if you're feeling convicted for your abusive conduct towards the people of God, my question to you is, "What are you going to do about it?" You have sinned openly against the Bride of Christ. Every time you embarrassed a brother or sister by correcting them in front of a group or destroyed a reputation by an open gossip, it was tantamount to exposing someone's nakedness in the open square. Does God treat you that way? Does he expose your hypocrisy by publicly shaming you? No, he does not. So, if you're feeling convicted for your abusive conduct, what do you do? You go to the people you hurt and begin with an apology! If the damage you've caused is so widespread that it's impossible to go to all the individuals you've hurt, then you make your apology as public as your abuse was.

Your next steps are extremely difficult. Although an apology is a tangible first step in repentance, it does not address the issue of your heart. The way you lead others is an expression of what you believe. The fact that you have abused the Bride of Christ in the ways mentioned in this book is proof of your beliefs. This cannot be fixed with an apology. At best, it's bad theology and likely impeachable character. You are going to need help. Depending upon the depths of your abuse, you may have to take some time off while getting this help. You will have to make yourself accountable to a group of men (preferably your elders) that have the authority to determine whether you are qualified to lead and when the Body of Christ would be safe in the event that you do return. You can be re-taught. The only question is whether you should be re-taught while remaining in a position to influence others.

There is no greater expression of love in scripture than the love God demonstrates toward his bride. The Bride of Christ's value is seen by what God was willing to pay for her. He gave his son's life so that she would have a home with him for all eternity. You have assaulted the bride he died for! It is not a light thing! It is not something God ignores! It also is not an unforgivable sin. If you recognize what you've done, repent, and turn back to the Lord to be taught what love looks like, he will forgive you! He will restore and mend your heart. He may even return you to a place of leadership where you get the privilege of serving the people of God as a "nobody" while you give God the glory you once stole from him! I pray this is your end!

I began this letter by saying there is one of two reactions the abuser is having towards what they've read so far. The first is a reaction of conviction which I've just addressed. The other is the abuser, who experiences no reaction because you don't see yourself as a perpetrator, therefore, your abuse is perpetual. Nothing is going to change because you think yourself to be the victim, all the while others are suffering from your abuse. I would like to speak to you now.

I need to preface what I'm about to say, as it may seem harsh at first glance. It might even seem as though it lacks the love of God one would expect to find in correction, so let me preface my words with this: this is not a correction. It is a stern rebuke and a warning that is substantiated by the only authority given to the church—The Word of God!

The people of faith have always suffered harm under the hand of Godless leaders whose narcissistic tendencies looked for self-gratification rather than God's glorification. This carnal pursuit of the heart is seen as early as Genesis 4 when Cain murdered Abel. It continues in Pharoah's massacre (Ex 1:22), Korah's rebellion (Num 16), Saul's jealousy (1 Sam 18:8), Haman's lust for recognition (Esther 3:5), Herod's sin (Matt 2), and so on. The Bible is replete with examples of people whose desire for self-aggrandizement brought death to others. This kind of premeditated abuse is more than bad leadership, it's demonic. It cares nothing for people, only the self.

It's the same heart seen by Lucifer in Isaiah 14:13, where pride sought after a position higher than the one that had been given.

You find yourself in the same company! You have used the church and the bride that Jesus died for to bring glory to yourself. To boost your ego and satisfy your lust for power. When you don't get the glory you believe you should, you pursue the righteous like Saul pursued David. You destroy any person who you perceive to be a threat to your authority, just like Pharoah and Herod. When people won't honor you the way you believe they should, you conspire like Haman to bring ruin to their lives. Your gossip moves through the congregation, causing the same division that Korah and his friends did, bringing a plague upon the people of God. And in the wake of your ruin, you shrug your shoulders, with not an ounce of regret, while blaming your spiritual carnage on the ones lying dead! This is not the heart of a shepherd. It is not the heart of God!

As I mentioned earlier, you might be tempted to interpret this portion of the letter as less than loving. So, to assure you of the Biblical fidelity behind what I'm saying, I would call your attention to the following passages:

> "The word of the LORD came to me: "Son of man, prophesy against the shepherds of Israel; prophesy, and say to them, even to the shepherds, Thus says the Lord GOD: Ah, shepherds of Israel who have been feeding yourselves! Should not shepherds feed the sheep? You eat the fat, you clothe yourselves with the wool, you slaughter the fat ones, but you do not feed the sheep. The weak you have not strengthened, the sick you have not healed, the injured you have not bound up, the strayed you have not brought back, the lost you have not sought, and with force and harshness, you have ruled them. So they were scattered because there was no shepherd, and they became food for all the wild beasts. My sheep were scattered; they wandered over all the mountains and on every high hill. My sheep were scattered over all the face of the earth, with none to search or seek for them.
>
> "Therefore, you shepherds, hear the word of the LORD: As I live, declares the Lord GOD, surely because my sheep have become a prey, and my sheep have become food for all the wild beasts since there was no shepherd, and because my shepherds have not searched for my sheep, but the shepherds have fed themselves, and have not fed my sheep, therefore, you shepherds, hear the word of the LORD: Thus says the

Lord GOD, Behold, I am against the shepherds, and I will require my sheep at their hand and put a stop to their feeding the sheep. No longer shall the shepherds feed themselves. I will rescue my sheep from their mouths, that they may not be food for them.

"For thus says the Lord GOD: Behold, I, I myself will search for my sheep and will seek them out. As a shepherd seeks out his flock when he is among his sheep that have been scattered, so will I seek out my sheep, and I will rescue them from all places where they have been scattered on a day of clouds and thick darkness. And I will bring them out from the peoples and gather them from the countries and will bring them into their own land. And I will feed them on the mountains of Israel, by the ravines, and in all the inhabited places of the country. I will feed them with good pasture, and on the mountain heights of Israel shall be their grazing land. There they shall lie down in good grazing land, and on rich pasture, they shall feed on the mountains of Israel. I myself will be the shepherd of my sheep, and I myself will make them lie down, declares the Lord GOD. I will seek the lost, and I will bring back the strayed, and I will bind up the injured, and I will strengthen the weak, and the fat and the strong I will destroy.[a] I will feed them in justice." –Ezekiel 34:1-16

I would like to highlight some of Ezekiel's "woes to the shepherds" of Israel. To begin with, God clearly establishes that he is "against the shepherds" (v.2,10). Why is God against them? We're told in v.2 because the shepherds had been feeding themselves. He nuances this in v.3 by saying the shepherds ate the best food and wore the best clothing. In other words, they used their position to take from the people. Perhaps they "casually" made their "needs" known so the people would feel sorry for them and give them their desires. We don't know, but we do know that they were taking advantage of the congregation. This is what happened with Eli's worthless sons. 1 Samuel 2:12 says that Eli's sons didn't know God and as a result, they were stealing from the boiling pots of meat. The boiling pots cooked the offerings that the people gave to God. It also says that they used their position to prey on the women servants. They were using the respect associated with their office to captivate the woman and have sex with them. In like manner, through your abuse, you have taken advantage of good-hearted people who trust the position you occupy. Some of you are guilty of the sins of Eli's sons. You use your position to prey on the opposite sex. Some of you use your position to steal or waste the offering. To protect yourself, you project on others the sins you are guilty of. You lie about others to draw attention away from your own immorality, your own theft. You point out the ruin in the marriages of others, while yours is held together with intimidation and threats, amounting to nothing more than a heap of ashes. You rule over people using fear as your weapon, supposing they will bow to your every request and acknowledge the fallacy of your spiritual superiority. You bully people with scripture, counting on their lack of knowledge or lack of spiritual stamina to fight back with the truth. You take advantage of the passive and malign the aggressive. Through the demonic influence of your manipulation, you convince people to live in your dark reality. Once they do, you cunningly suggest that loyalty to you is tantamount to loyalty to God. You present yourself to be knowledgeable in all things. You're a doctor when people talk about health. You're a lawyer when matters of law come up. You're a theologian when matters of faith are spoken of. All this, and more so that you can be the center of every conversation. You are always the teacher and never the learner. You are always right, never wrong, and through your ability to articulate, along with your well-mannered behavior, you convince your followers you're holy. Yet, behind closed doors, your true self is seen. The people closest to you are a constant reminder of the fragility of the image you have sold to others. Insecurity is what you lie down with and what you wake up to. You have lied to friends, family, and most of all-God. And the Lord sees it all!

In addition to taking advantage of the people, we're told the shepherds ruled with "force and harshness." The word "harshness" means "to break apart" or "fracture." Notice, they "ruled" the people, they didn't serve them! They ruled them by fracturing them or breaking them down. God was against this. When you use condemnation to control a person, you show yourself to be the same harsh ruler that God opposes. When you attempt to break people down or fracture them by humiliation, God recoils. When you publicly have people confess their sin in front of the congregation and then call it "a beautiful picture of repentance," you show the harshness of the shepherds of Israel living in your heart! When have you ever publicly declared your sin without it first being found out? Why don't you hold yourself to the same standards you impose on those you lead? In Matthew 23:4, Jesus said of the Pharisees:

> *"They tie up heavy burdens hard to bear and lay them on people's shoulders, but they themselves are not willing to move them with their finger."*

A double standard in leadership is condemned by God. You don't get a hall pass protecting you against gossip when you're talking to your staff or congregants. You're bound by the same standards they are.

So, what's next for you? I'm sure that in your mind you think all is well and you'll continue as usual. It's what you've done for years. Well, I have some bad news for you. God saw everything and continues to see everything. Since God is not mocked and man will eventually reap what he sows (Galatians 6:7), you are clearly not getting away with anything. In Ecclesiastes 8:11, Solomon says:

> *"Because the sentence against an evil deed is not executed speedily, the heart of the children of men is fully set to do evil."*

What this means is that you have likely mistaken the patience of God for the mercy of God. In the face of this mistake, you're continuing on with the false assumption that God is for you and looks the other way at your abuse. Your heart is, as Solomon said, "fully set to do evil." However, your error will be your undoing. God's patience and God's mercy are very different. God's mercy pertaining to our sin is always given on the heels of repentance. This is what Isaiah was talking about in Isaiah 55:5-7 when he said:

> *"Seek the Lord while he may be found; call upon him while he is near; let the wicked forsake their way, and the unrighteous man his thoughts; let him return to the Lord that he may have mercy on him, and to our God, for he will abundantly pardon him."*

Notice that God's pardon is partnered with his mercy which is contingent upon a person forsaking their wicked way and returning to God. We call that "repentance," therefore, without repentance, there is no mercy. However, the patience of God fills the gap between the time an offense is committed and the time a person repents of it. This is what Peter was referring to in 2 Peter 3:9 when he said:

> *"The Lord is not slow to fulfill his promise, as some count slowness, but is patient toward you, not wishing that any should perish, but that all should reach repentance."*

Once again, notice that the patience spoken of by Peter lies in the gap between a person's offense and their repentance. The patience is extended so that a person can have the opportunity to repent and not suffer judgement. The difference between patience and mercy is that "mercy endures forever (Ps 136)," whereas patience ends at judgement.

What does this mean for you, the abuser? It's simple since you refuse to acknowledge your sin against the Bride of Christ and the spiritual abuse you have dealt out to so many, it's impossible to repent. You don't see the need. Therefore, the patience of God you are experiencing will run out and give way to God's judgement. Whether that judgement comes in the form of a believer's chastisement, because, "God chastises every son whom he receives (Heb 12:6)," or whether it comes to you as an unbeliever made up to look like a believer, it will come.

How does a person in your position, having influence over others, avoid the tidal wave of judgement coming their way? To be honest, I'm not sure. The seriousness of beating the Bride of Christ in ignorance is one thing, to do it with premeditation is something completely different. I do know this judgement was on its way to Nineveh when they took seriously the warning handed down by the prophet. It wasn't too late for them. They repented and God stayed his hand. In the same way, the size and darkness of the tidal wave headed your way is certain. Perhaps a lesson from Jonah could be heeded? The King of Nineveh, a godless man, heard the warning from Jonah and sent a message to the kingdom saying:

> *"Let everyone turn from his evil way and from the violence of his hands. Who knows? God may turn and relent from his fierce anger so that* we may *not perish (Jonah 3:8)."*

There is such a thing as going too far and not listening to the Lord's voice, where judgement becomes unavoidable. Manasseh found this out the hard way. God spoke and he wouldn't listen, so the Lord brought him into the chains of his enemy, then he cried out in repentance.

You have caused great damage to the Body of Christ! You have devoured them as a wolf breaking into the sheep pin and slaughtering the innocent. Despite your education or your knowledge of the Bible, the fruit of your effectiveness as a shepherd is seen in the trail of ruin that follows you. Yet, the Bible knows your kind well and foretells your future when in Proverbs 26:24-28 it says:

> *Whoever hates disguises himself with his lips and harbors deceit in his heart; when he speaks graciously, believe him not, for there are seven abominations in his heart; though his hatred be*

> *covered with deception, his wickedness will be exposed in the assembly. Whoever digs a pit will fall into it, and a stone will come back on him who starts it rolling. A lying tongue hates its victims, and a flattering mouth works ruin.*

"...his wickedness will be exposed in the assembly." Those are the words that I pray follow you everywhere you go. I pray that these words create a fear of the Lord that is absent in you, seen by your treatment of Christ's bride. I pray that this fear of the Lord drives you to recognize your need to repent of the hatred you've disguised with your lips. If you choose not to repent, then your exposure to the assembly will be certain. It will be as Jesus said:

> *For in the same way you judge others, you will be judged, and with the measure you use, it will be measured to you. –Matthew 7:2*

When I began this letter, I said that it would seem harsh and seem unloving at times but that it would be rooted in scripture. You should be careful not to dismiss what I'm saying because you find the directness to be appalling. God saves some of his harshest words for the abusers of his people. In Matthew 23:15, Jesus told the religious Pharisees this:

> *"Woe to you scribes and Pharisees, Hypocrites! For you travel across sea and land to make a single proselyte, and when he becomes a proselyte, you make him twice as much a child of hell as yourselves."*

Again, in Matthew 23:13, he says:

> *"Woe to you, scribes and Pharisees, hypocrites! For you shut the kingdom of heaven in people's faces. For you neither enter yourselves nor allow those, who would enter to go in."*

In both these cases, Jesus uses the harshest of words for leaders who are inside the "church" but outside the kingdom. These People were leading in such a way that their abuse had eternal ramifications for their victims. Over and over in the Old Testament, God is direct in addressing evil and abusive leaders. He does not mix passivity with his directness. There is no ambiguity when he addresses them. Jeremiah 23:1-11 says:

> *"Woe to the shepherds who destroy and scatter my sheep... you have scattered my flock and have driven them away... I will attend to your evil deeds... both prophet and priest are ungodly in my house, I have found their evil."*

God is jealous for his bride. Faithful shepherds understand this. Faithful shepherds walk with a particular sensitivity to rightly representing the Lord's heart towards his people. It is the highest calling to treat God's people the way he commands.

So again, I urge you to repent for your abuse. Step down and get help. The church of God is gracious and merciful. They will extend to you what you weren't willing to give to them. They will love you in spite of your treatment of them. Your apologies will help some heal and might bring restoration to damaged relationships. It is a painful path as it will require brokenness that you have yet to show you possess. However, it's the path that honors God and best demonstrates the shepherd's heart that you claim to have, or you can do nothing. You can hold your ground and claim your innocence. You can surround yourself with a new group of leaders and new congregants ignorant of who you really are. You can begin the process of abuse all over again. However, at some point, your last wave will arrive, and you will be no more. I urge you to choose the former, for your sake and for the sake of Christ's church!

In His Name,

Steve

Conclusion

My greatest hope for you is that by reading this account of so many people's experiences, you will have what's necessary to protect yourself from the harm which comes from spiritual abuse. The damage to the mind and heart is real. The scars often run so deep that healing can seem impossible at times. Emotions can lead a person to dark places where hatred rules the tongue and love is almost unrecognizable. My prayer is that by reading this book, you will know that you are not alone. Your situation is unique to you, but it's not unique to the body of Christ. Take comfort in knowing that many people share your same pain and have agonized over what they now see in their rearview mirror. I pray that you do not hold the whole of Christianity responsible for the actions of a few. My prayer is that you realize that man is responsible for your hurt, not God. God wants to use this suffering and injustice to refine portions of your life. If you let him, he will bring you through this with a greater appreciation for church leadership, not a disdain for it. You see, once you are able to identify what abuse is, care becomes so much sweeter! The leadership of Christ, as seen through caring and loving shepherds, will be unmistakably clear to you.

It may seem that your faith journey has stalled due to your abuse. However, can I encourage you with a reality you are not yet privy to? God never wastes suffering! What may seem like a stall to you today is actually preparation for who you're going to help tomorrow! Someone is going through the very things you are. Some are just beginning their trauma and have no idea of the damage awaiting them. You'll be their help. You'll be the one God uses to bring them back from their despair. So, to that end, I say, keep going! The Lord is your strong tower!

Made in the USA
Columbia, SC
17 September 2024